HOW TO BOWL FASTER

...and take more wickets!

Paul Hoffmann

LHM

ISBN: 9798698839385

Cover design by: Joshua Johnston (Twitter: @Josh_EK11)
Back cover art by: Craig Smith (Instagram: @smitt23)
Images courtesy of:
donaldmacleod.com (Twitter: @clanmacleod)
David Potter (Twitter: @DMP_Dunfermline)
Barry Chambers (cricketeurope.com)
Library of Congress Control Number: 2018675309
Printed in the United States of America

To my parents, Tony and Margaret, who encouraged me to play sport from a young age.

CONTENTS

Title Page   1

Copyright   2

Dedication   3

Foreword   9

Introduction   11

"How can I bowl faster?"   17

Mental Strength and Attitude   21

A Lesson from Mike Whitney   30

You Can't Control the Uncontrollable   34

How Kylie Minogue Helped the Aussies win the 1999 World   40
Cup

Buy the right Footwear and feel the immediate benefit   43

How to Generate Power and Accuracy with a Standard   46
Seam Grip

The Outswinger   51

The Inswinger   54

The Leg-Cutter   58

The Off-Cutter   60

Cross-Seam   62

Slower Ball Variations   64

I Bowled an Absolute 'Pie' to Shane Watson in the 2007   68

World Cup

Getting the ball to Reverse Swing   71

How Do I Determine the Length of My Run-Up?   76

Getting told off by Sir Vivian Richards, and Fast Bowling   80
Fraudsters at the Gabba

Chats with Craig McDermott, and Finding Your Perfect   85
Approach to the Crease

Get Your Limbs Working in Unison   93

Fixing a Collapsed Back Leg   104

How to prevent Falling Over at Delivery   108

Drills to Improve Your Accuracy   117

A Tip on Finding the Edge of the Bat   121

Generate Maximum Wrist Snap   126

Tactics Overview   129

Tactics for a Batsman 'Playing it Safe'   131

Bodyline   136

How to Bowl to an Attacking Batsman   138

New Ball Tactics to an Attacking Batsman   140

Setting a Field for the new ball   146

Death Bowling   151

Setting a Field for Death Bowling   163

Develop Good Training Habits   165

The Day of the Match   168

Fitness   170

Off-Season Cardiovascular Fitness Programme (gym   172
members)

Off-Season Strength Programme (gym members)   174

Off-Season Cardiovascular Activities (non-gym   177
members)

Off-Season Strength Exercises (no gym)   179

Fitness Activities During the Season   183

Diet   185

Respect the Umpires   190

Ignore the boundary experts   194

Respect the game and Don't shoulder barge batsmen.   197

Conclusion   204

Acknowledgement   209

About The Author   211

Books By This Author   213

Miscellaneous   215

FOREWORD

by David Kelso

He was the Rockhampton Rocket who became a Queensland Quickie and the Lanarkshire Lightning who became a Scotland Speed Merchant.

Many top class cricketers have come to Caledonia to ply their trade - but few, if any, have left the impression made by Hoffy.

Not only was he a veritable giant on the field with Uddingston and the Saltires, he was and still is one of the most affable and engaging personalities you will ever come across off it.

Paul was a World Cup level performer who was also a leading light in the early years of the century when the Scots frequently claimed the scalps of the English Counties and rival ICC Associate nations.

Hoffy's love for Scotland and its people was underlined by his decision to settle and set up home there in the wake of a spell back in Queensland.

His birthright will always be Australian, however as far as any Scot is concerned, he is one of us.

Now teacher of English with one book already under his belt, he embarked on this offering, and it is hard to imagine anyone more suitable to write on the topic of fast bowling. It is a marvellous delivery.

* David Kelso is a renowned sports journalist and a passionate

supporter of both Scottish rugby and cricket.

INTRODUCTION

*"...I loved the loud fizz of the ball
as it thundered into the hard, black
rubber matting behind the stumps."*

I knew I wanted to be a fast bowler when, as a wide-eyed young boy, I would stand in a side net and watch George Brabon bowl. George who?

George Brabon played for Frenchville in my hometown of Rock-hampton, and he also represented Queensland six times, once dismissing Geoff Boycott at the Gabba for single figures.

My Dad, Tony, was an all-rounder for Frenchville in the '70s and early '80s. I would bowl at his teammates, but when I took a rest, I took great pleasure in watching batsmen squirm when facing Brabon. Standing just a few metres from the batsmen, I loved the loud fizz of the ball as it thundered into the hard, black rubber matting behind the stumps.

FRENCHVILLE CRICKET CLUB

A GRADE PREMIERS 1978-79

Back Row :— J. O'DONNELL, D. DAHL, G. BRABON, D. McBRYDE, T. HOFFMAN, B. BIDGOOD.
Front Row :— R. HIELSCHER, B. HARTLEY, W. SOUTER (Capt.), S. SAVAGE, D. EVERETT.
Absent :— M. CROSS.

Frenchville Cricket Club in Rockhampton, Australia. Includes George Brabon and my father, Tony Hoffmann.

The look on each batsman's face was one of terror as if each Brabon ball was a life or death moment. Somewhat worryingly, I wanted to have that power that Brabon had. The speed to turn batsmen's legs into lettuce. Bowling, in tandem with George, at the age of eight, was the moment my love affair with fast bowling began.

My other inspiration was the great Aussie quick, Dennis Lillee. When Lillee bowled, I was glued to the TV. I was in awe of his artistry: the smooth yet brisk run-up, with locks of thinning hair bouncing with every stride and his flared white trousers flapping, as he approached the crease with determination in his eyes.

One day in the early 1980s, my Dad took my older brother and me to a World Series Cup game at the Gabba. I can't remember who Australia was playing.

All I remember from our side-on view from the old dog track was the sight of 'DK' Lillee taking off from his long run-up, his trouser flares and the frightening speed of the ball as it thudded into Rodney Marsh's gloves a good 20 yards back from the batsman.

Viv Richards was incredible to watch with the willow, but I wanted to be a fast bowler. I wanted to be the next 'DK' Lillee.

In fierce backyard battles with my older brother, Craig, I would pretend to be 'DK', flicking off forehead sweat with my index finger, setting off from the mulberry fruit tree, arms pumping back and forth as I gathered momentum across my Dad's proud paspalum lawn to the makeshift crease, eyes continually locked on the target ahead.

My bound before release was extravagant. My head tilted to the side, while my left hand sprawled out as it thrust into the sky.

I continued with an overly long follow-through down the cut pitch, with a steely glare at my brother. A final flick of forehead sweat completed the ritual.

The violent sound of the ball, like a shotgun blast, thudding into the keeper - an orange trampoline tipped over to its side - was a thing of beauty.

I didn't care so much about getting my brother out. I just wanted to bowl fast. Like Brabon. Like Lillee.

Unfortunately, I was never able to reach the speeds of a prime 'DK'. If I did, I might have fulfilled the dream of wearing the Baggy Green cap.

The backyard battles with my Dad and older brother was the only time I was able to wear the 'Baggy Green'. However, when I take time out to reminisce, I did ok: Queensland Country, Australia Country (that was a Baggy Green of sorts) and 119 official caps Scotland were some of my highlights.

With over 30 years of experience, in contrasting conditions, under some of the finest cricketing brains and fitness coaches in world cricket, I've made it my duty to absorb as much information as possible.

I've also learned on my feet, picking up nuances, skills and tactics for every possible game scenario. Fast bowling has been my obsession since I was a kid growing up in a North Rockhampton bungalow.

While playing at Bethesda Cricket Club in North Wales in 1994, I recall an old teammate Iain Buchanan propping up the bar, describing fast bowlers as the rock stars of a cricket team - the individuals who attract all the groupies, painting us as lothario like figures.

But, funnily enough, I've never thought of it like that.

Dedicated fast bowlers are too wrapped up in their 'art' and statistics to concern themselves with outside distractions.

We are the archetypal alpha character, born to wreak havoc, to intimidate batsmen and to revel in being worshipped by those who wanted to bowl quick, but just couldn't.

Many batsmen at training have whined: "I wish I could bowl fast - I'd just bowl bouncers every ball!". The fascination is purely about speed and destruction.

At coaching sessions, the most often asked question from young quicks is not related to run-ups, techniques or seam positioning. It's: "How can I bowl faster?"'

Throughout this book, I delve deep into every aspect of the skill, from footwear, seam position, your approach and delivery, as well as targeted drills to improve speed and accuracy.

I also examine different bowling plans for various match scenarios, including how to set your field to maximise these plans.

In addition to this, I will also promote physical exercise that will maximise your output, take a close look at nutrition to help aid performance and discuss the mental side of the game and how to remain calm in the most stressful of scenarios.

No stone is left unturned in my quest to tap into the vast pool of potential quicks out there.

Whether it's converting a lower grade 'pie-thrower' into a fearsome wicket-taking machine, or just adding a half of pace onto an already brisk bowler, this book will have something for every bowler who wants to improve.

As the curtain draws on my career as a fast bowler, I have a burning desire to share with other inspiring quicks - young or old - what I have learnt throughout my time on the pitch.

☐ Parkana speedster Paul Hoffman (pictured) pins down another Brothers batsmer while on his way to the impressive figures of 3/41 off 23 overs in Parkana's win or Saturday.
B73/3C

Playing for my club Parkana in Rockhampton in 1991.
Dennis Lillee inspired the long hair and flared trousers.

"HOW CAN I BOWL FASTER?"

The answer to this million-dollar question? Well, that's not so straightforward, but throughout this book, I will explore how we can achieve that extra yard of pace.

Most fast bowlers are born. Some have the potential to bowl fast, but just don't know it yet.

The fastest bowlers have unique traits and physical attributes to help them bowl well above 90mph.

Think of Jeff Thompson, the Australian tearaway from the '70's and early '80's. His natural javelin style action was a thing of beauty that can't be coached.

Curtly Ambrose, the tall West Indian quick from the '80's and '90's, had a natural snap of wrist at the point of delivery, as did Andrew Flintoff and more recently, Dale Steyn.

Shoaib Akhtar, arguably the quickest ever, generated pace from a combination of run-up speed, muscle and a unique slinging action.

Latterly, Jasprit Bumrah of India has an uncoachable hyper-extension in his bowling arm. This flex allows him to hurl deliveries down at high speed, despite a short, stop-start approach, much like a gazelle bounding across the African plains.

Jasprit Bumrah's excessive hyperextension helps him generate speeds of up to 90mph.

For us mere mortals, bowling over 90mph is only a dream. But is it? Is it possible to make changes to your training and technique that will add speed to your deliveries?

Whether or not you'll be able to reach 90mph depends on how quickly you can bowl now. If you're a medium-pacer, then I do not doubt that a yard of extra pace is achievable.

Some adjustments can be made that will help increase speed significantly.

I once read an article that said Jason Gillespie was a medium pace trundler in the bowels of Adelaide grade cricket before he began taking the sport seriously, and discovered he could bowl quick.

As hard as I tried, I could never be an express bowler. I didn't have the athleticism or suppleness to reach speeds above 90mph. I was, however, quick enough to make life uncomfortable for batsmen, especially in the period between my late teens to my early 20's.

Back pain robbed me of the disconcerting pace I had in those years. Instead, I evolved into a dependable line and length bowler who relied primarily on accuracy and seam movement, but with enough speed to keep batsmen honest.

There's no doubt that coaching strategies, body management and strength and conditioning drills targeted at fast bowlers have developed a great deal since I was a young tearaway. If I was able to apply the strategies and fitness routines outlined in this book when I was at my peak, I might have been able to bowl quicker for many more years.

The shift for a quick bowler is not easy. It requires a lot of hard physical work, diligence as well as a good dose of patience and dedication to the skill.

But, the rewards for bowling fast are irresistible. Batsmen fear you. Teammates worship you. Fast bowlers are the hitmen of the cricket team, the individuals who are out there to set the tone - to assert authority.

Life as a fast bowler is fulfilling, providing you're performing to your optimum potential.

**Scotland fast bowler, John Blain, in action
against Ireland in 2005.**
(Image courtesy of Barry Chambers cricketeurope.com)

MENTAL STRENGTH AND ATTITUDE

Scotland and Warwickshire legend Dougie Brown
(Image courtesy of Cricket Scotland)
"I would get the bus from London to Stirling on Friday evening and play for Clackmannanshire on the weekend, and then go back to University in London for a Monday morning lecture. I was desperate to play cricket for Scotland, so that's why I kept coming

back to play for Clackmannan." Dougie Brown.

In 2003, my old Scottish teammate, Dougie Brown, told me a great story when we shared a room in Sharjah.

I asked him how he managed to get a contract at Warwickshire County Cricket Club, a juggernaut of English cricket.

He said he invited himself for a trial by writing a letter to Warwickshire - much like Paul Wilson did in the early '90s to get into the Australian Institute of Sport Cricket Academy.

On the day of the trial, Dougie knew within himself that there were more talented players, quicker bowlers and more flamboyant batsmen.

To him, it didn't matter a jot, because while other trialists faded in the Birmingham heat as the day wore on, Dougie kept charging in, giving it everything and maintaining the same intensity he had displayed at the start.

"It was a boiling hot day at Edgbaston. There were 13 of us. It was a bit of a test - they put down jugs of ice-cold water and juice, basically to see who would stop first. So, I did what I always did - I kept running in and running in. Warwickshire invited me to a second trial with two others who had come through the system from an early age. Bob Cottom then called me a week later and told me that Warwickshire wanted to offer me a £130 a week summer contract. I was like, "I'd do this for nothing...because it wasn't about the cash, it was about grabbing the opportunity"." Dougie Brown.

This mental fortitude, hunger and intense self-belief in what was effectively a gruelling cricketing boot camp is what secured Dougie the contract.

The Warwickshire scouts knew they had someone to work with, an individual with an enduring work ethic and someone who was never going to give up, no matter what is thrown at him.

This wonderful anecdote is a lesson for all aspiring quicks. Talent can only take you so far.

"There's no secret to the success of great sportspeople. They do that little bit extra."

During that tour in Sharjah, Dougie would get up early in the morning and go for a casual four-mile run, even on the day of a game. I was tired just thinking about it.

Then Dougie told me about the former South African fast bowler, Makhaya Ntini. Ntini ran at least five miles every morning, even on the mornings of a test match.

Ntini was a bowler who kept running in, maintaining pace, while the bowling speed of his peers dropped as the day wore on.

Like Ntini, Dougie never sat still. He always pushed himself to be better, even in the latter stages of his career. He never cut corners.

There's no secret to the success of great sportspeople. They do that little bit extra.

When training finishes, they'll stay back and work on a specific skill - they'll stay back and physically challenge themselves further.

Or, like Dougie, they'll get up at the crack of dawn, and churn out a few miles. In hindsight, I probably lacked Dougie's constant and disciplined work ethic. I pushed myself, but not as often as I could have.

"I hated every minute of training, but I said, 'Don't quit. Suffer now and live the rest of

your life as a champion." Muhammad Ali.

I'm not a big one for inspirational quotes, but one quote that reson-ated with me was this one by Muhammad Ali.

It's a quote that, as a teacher, I have on a poster, in my classroom. I never wanted to cut corners, but sometimes I did because hard work is challenging.

> *"He doesn't cut corners, and*
> *he goes above and beyond*
> *what is asked of him."*

If I skipped a session at the gym, and then underperformed in a game that weekend, my apathy riddled me with guilt.

When I read about Steve Smith punishing himself by running back to the team hotel if he fails with the bat, I can understand why he does it. He expects the best from himself. There is a reason why he's currently the world's best batsman. He doesn't cut corners, and he goes above and beyond what is asked of him.

My former opening bowling partner, John Blain, is now an English Cricket Board (ECB) Level 4 coach and the Director of Cricket at the Grange Cricket Academy in Edinburgh.

As a respected mentor for aspiring quicks, John will assess the tech-nical side of their actions to iron out any kinks.

Aside from external strengths and flaws, what John looks for in a young fast bowler is desire.

John Blain, former Scotland, Yorkshire and Northamptonshire professional and Cricket Scotland Hall of Fame inductee 2019.
(Image courtesy of Barry Chambers cricketeurope.com)

"Above all else, what coaches want to see is desire. Fast bowling requires a lot of hard work and dedication. I want to see a desire to keep improving, to push themselves physically and to ask questions. Unless that desire is there,

coaching becomes more difficult." John Blain.

Training hard isn't always fun. It's not much fun bowling on lifeless pitches or in 35-degree heat. However, pushing your body to the limits knowing there are goals and rewards at the end, whether it be the euphoria of a five-wicket haul or a contribution to a team win, is the fuel that keeps you going when you might want to quit.

"Rixon made me bat in a net that included two of Australia's most hostile and intimidating quicks."

Steve Rixon gave me a tough test in my first New South Wales training session at the SCG nets in 1993. It was an initiation to test my courage in the most daunting of situations.

He told me to pad up at the start of the session. Pad up? I was a tailender! Surely I should be batting at the end of a session? Here I am, looking like I've just stepped out of my Holden Commodore, wearing a South Sydney Rabbitohs rugby league jersey and a pair of shorts. New South Wales had yet to provide me with any training kit. Rixon made me bat in a net that included two of Australia's most hostile and intimidating quicks: Wayne 'Cracker' Holdsworth and the 6'9" left-arm paceman, Phil Alley.

I'd never met these blokes before now. I'd only seen them peppering batsmen on television, batsmen that were much more capable and skilful than me.

Holdsworth was Australia's quickest bowler at the time, possibly in the world. You only have to watch old clips of him online to see that he probably bowled 90+mph consistently.

"I did the unthinkable and charged him first ball."

And, as I stood there waiting for him to hurl a thunderbolt into my ribs, I wondered why his nickname was 'Cracker'. Did he have a temper? Who knows, but I did the unthinkable and charged him first ball. My reasoning? Rixon wanted to test me. I'm sure of it. But, I've never been one to back down from a scrap. I wanted to come back twice as hard.

The fact that I failed to connect was neither here nor there. I didn't back away. I knew I was being tested, and if I failed the test, it would've made a lasting impression on Rixon.

Fast bowlers should be equipped, mentally and physically, to deal with whatever situation that confronts them.

I've recently had conversations with Shane Burger, the current coach of the Scotland men's team and a former South African first-class player. Shane was a respected all-round cricketer who was capable of bowling express spells in the oppressive humidity of his home country.

Shane famously clean bowled Sachin Tendulkar in a T20 Champions League match in South Africa. Now, a top coach, he told me what he looks for in a fast bowler.

"I would like to see a fast bowler with the ability to bowl quick all day, with an element of skill that can be developed. A fast bowler who has passion and a big heart - and - a fast bowler who is resilient with a strong mentality. They can bowl on flat pitches and keep coming in all day - even if they're getting hit." Shane Burger.

Dougie Brown ticked those boxes. Makhaya Ntini ticked those boxes. All the great fast bowlers tick those boxes. The dedication they have for the skill allows them to perform in the toughest of conditions.

*"Keep improving while
others are resting."*

Just as top-class batsmen will dig in on a difficult pitch, great fast bowlers will keep running in and hitting the deck hard on the most unresponsive of pitches.

Elite sportspeople will keep working hard and will never give in. My best advice? Be the fittest version of yourself. Run the extra mile when training. Keep improving while others are resting. When you're playing, want the ball. Beg the captain if you have to.

I was fortunate enough to play under captains such as Craig Wright, Ricky Bawa and Bryan Clarke, who backed my skills because I always put my hand up, and on most occasions, I never let them down.

Make the most of your opportunity and don't give your skipper the chance to take you off.

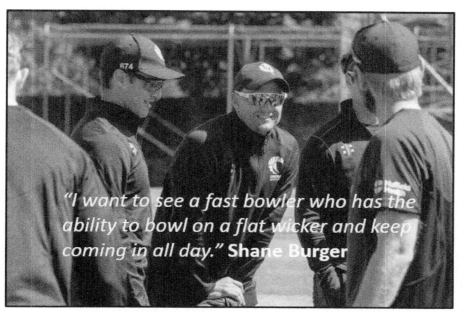

Scotland coach and former South African first-class player, Shane Burger.

(Image courtesy of donald-macleod.com)

A LESSON FROM MIKE WHITNEY

Former New South Wales and Australian
Fast Bowler, Mike Whitney
(Image courtesy of Fairfax Media Australia)

"Don't you ever let me hear you
say you've had enough!"

I learnt a career-changing lesson when I was playing in a 1993 preseason warm-up game at Hawkesbury Cricket Club in Richmond, a suburb in north-west Sydney.

It was a mix of New South Wales Sheffield Shield squad players - some superstars of Australian cricket, and some up and coming talent who were pushing for state selection.

My captain was the barrel-chested, no-nonsense, curly-haired left-arm quick Mike Whitney. Whitney had played for Australia and was a New South Wales cricket legend.

I had bowled four overs with the new ball and was holding my own against the elite of Sydney cricket. Whitney approached me before my fifth over and asked:

'How are you travelling? Do you want this
to be your last over in the spell?'

It was a stinking hot day, and the pitch was an absolute road. I was keen to protect my figures of 1-9, so I nodded my head and said 'yeah ok'.

I was a little overawed by Whitney. Only a month before this, I had been lounging in the family house in Rockhampton, stuffing my face with banana sandwiches and chocolate malt drinks.

Now, here I was, talking to Mike Whitney, bowling to Michael Slater and sharing the new ball with Glenn McGrath. It was as if I was living in some kind of weird dream.

Mentally, I probably wasn't prepared for the sudden step up in level. But I never struggled with the ball in hand. This skill was due to a finely tuned muscle memory, forged from years of bowling at backyard targets in Rockhampton.

Anyhow, Whitney's response was blunt.

> *'Listen! Don't you ever let me hear you say you've had enough! If me or any other captain you play under ask if you want to keep going, you tell them, 'yes, I'll keep going until you tell me to stop!'*

I might have missed a few expletives in his retort, but from that day, when a skipper asked me that question, I would tell them that I wanted to keep bowling.

The moral of the story? Don't give the impression you're willing to give up easily. Keep wanting to bowl. As my old Rockhampton captain and coach 'Jock' Carroll once said:

> *"...you can't get batsmen out if you're not bowling."*

My former Rockhampton captain and coach, John 'Jock' Carroll.

YOU CAN'T CONTROL
THE UNCONTROLLABLE

"...even the most skilful and hard-working quicks are vulnerable to getting punished."

Bad luck is inevitable in life - as is good luck. I've experienced my share of both with cricket.

A 'sliding doors' moment for me was In January 1992 at an awards night in Newcastle, Australia, after the Australian Country Cricket Carnival. I had been named in the Australian team and remembered having a conversation with a gentleman named Brian Gainsford. Brian was involved with Manly Warringah Cricket Club and he suggested that I could possibly play for the Sydney club.

Brian's son, David, was a first-grade regular and his daughter, Melinda, was an Australian sprinter who represented the nation in the Commonwealth and Olympic Games.

That would be difficult, because I lived in Rockhampton, a two-day drive north of Sydney. I didn't entertain the idea, not until a few weeks later when I was playing for my club in Rockhampton, Parkana. It was a 'lightbulb moment'. If I was to progress, I had to do something. So, I got back in touch with Brian and he passed my details to the Manly President, Gary Flowers.

After some discussions with Gary, the club then flew me to Sydney and put me up with the club secretary, Bob Brenner. After a few games in second-grade, I got picked for the first grade team, captained by Phil Marks. I took five wickets in the first-grade semi-final against Randwick and then another nine wickets in the final against Northern Districts.

A few months later - after moving back to Rockhampton for the winter, I was named in the New South Wales Sheffield Shield squad for the 1993/94 season. If I hadn't had that conversation with Brian Gainsford, this meteoric rise would never have happened. But, I've had my share of bad luck too.

In 1993, I was on the verge of getting picked for the all-conquering New South Wales Sheffield Shield team. I'd taken plenty of wickets in first grade for Manly, and was successful in my games with the state's Second XI side, which included Adam Gilchrist.

After taking seven scalps in a fixture against Parramatta at King's Oval, I was told by insiders that I just needed another good performance and the selectors would have to pick me.

I was the most consistent performer with the ball in Sydney and when former Australian spinner Greg Matthews phoned me up one day to tell me that I was "the best fast bowler in Australia", I naively believe that, yep, maybe I was, although in reality Greg was trying to butter me up, as he wanted me to leave Manly and play for his club, Eastern Suburbs.

In my next game for Manly we played St George at Hurstville Oval. The unthinkable happened. For the first time in my career, I had torn an intercostal muscle. Not quite wanting to believe it, I foolishly tried to bowl another ball to Brad McNamara, the New South Wales all-rounder. The delivery was so slow it bounced a couple of times to Brad. He was kind enough to pat it away and told me to go off. I was out of action for five weeks. My moment had passed.

Later in the season, my form returned. I was finally selected in a New South Wales squad for a Sheffield Shield fixture. But, after bowling marathon spells for Manly, my shin splints had become far too painful to last a four-day game, so with a heavy heart, I made myself unavailable.

The following season I returned from a stint as a professional cricketer for Bethesda Cricket Club in North Wales. After months jogging and hiking around the peaks of Snowdonia National Park, I was fitter than I'd ever been. I began to build momentum with a string of wickets for Manly, and there was talk again about getting picked for New South Wales. In one early season game against North Sydney, I bowled a hostile spell, picking up a few wickets to help us win the game. Manly were top of the table.

The following game we travelled to the University of New South Wales. In the changing room, I was told by our manager that New South Wales selector Geoff Lawson was at the game to watch me.

Lawson was an excellent fast bowler for Australia in the early '80s. Suddenly, I felt under pressure to perform, and I bowled one of the worst spells I can remember. I tried to bowl too fast, struggled for rhythm and walked off wicketless. Lawson could not have been impressed with what he witnessed.

That was probably my last chance. I was 25 and at that age, with young quicks like Stuart Clark and Matt Nicholson coming through, I felt like I was already consigned to the fast bowling scrap heap. My performances dipped for a period of time after that, as I struggled with form and confidence. Bad luck happens and sometimes, life just doesn't turn out as you had planned.

If you're doing everything you possibly can to make yourself a better bowler, then don't feel too bad about the occasional bad spell, or taking the odd 'tanking', especially in a T20 game.

Sometimes, on a flat pitch, going for runs will happen, regardless of whether you're bowling to plan. You only have to look at how bowlers fare in the Indian Premier League to understand that even the most skilful and hard-working quicks are vulnerable to getting punished.

For example, in a recent One Day International series against England, Josh Hazlewood went for just 26 and 27 runs from his ten overs in games one and two respectively. Then, in the third and final fixture, he went wicketless and was hit for 68 from his ten overs. The games were all played at Old Trafford on flat, dry pitches.

Expect bad days at the office. It happens to the best.

If, for example, you nail your yorker, but you get scooped over the keeper, there's not much you can do about it. Return to your mark and know what delivery you're going to bowl next.

> *"I dealt with a lot of adversity in the early stages, but I persevered. If you're playing professional sport, you will have more bad days than good days, particularly cricket because a lot of the things you can't control - you can control your preparation and processes. Still, the outcomes you can't control, because there's always somebody likely to have one ball in them that's better than your day, and you have to deal with that. If you're resilient enough, you keep trying and keep pushing. Get yourself to the point where you deserve to get picked." Dougie Brown.*

At times, I struggled with nerves before a game - anxiety that stemmed from the thought of getting hit for runs, especially in the opening overs when my role was to establish authority and stability for my club sides and Scotland.

"...I hated the bus journey to the game and the pre-match warm-up drills."

Outwardly, I never showed nerves. I didn't want to reveal weakness. It was the worry of what could potentially happen, to the point where I hated the bus journey to the game and the pre-match warm-up drills.

I often felt tired and weak in the legs before a game, more because of nervous exhaustion than anything else. However, when I stood at the top of my mark with a new ball, negative thoughts disappeared. Later in my 20s, as back injuries robbed me of pace, I began to feel more like a pre-programmed droid, who knew exactly where to bowl and how to instinctively adapt to what the batsman was doing because, at training, I practised my yorkers. I drilled my back of the length 'hip-to-heart balls and I refined my subtle changes in seam positioning. I punished my legs with squats and always felt conditioned and prepared for battle. For the most part, I felt supremely confident in my skills.

What I struggled to come to terms with was a batsman who was able to get the better of me. A dasher who smashed me about the 'park': however, if I knew that deep down, I had prepared as diligently as possible, there was nothing much else I could do.

I can recall only one occasion where I felt helpless as a bowler. It was my final match for Scotland in the English domestic one-day competition. We were playing Worcestershire at New Road and I had travelled to Worcestershire the night before after a shift at work.

The pitch was barren and the boundaries were tiny. Vikram Solanki struck four boundaries in a row off me. It felt like that no matter where I bowled, I was going to get smashed. Luckily, he edged the fifth ball to third man after another almighty swing. I had never been so happy to get Graham Hick on strike. Aside from Merv Hughes, not many bowlers would have said that down the years!

Sometimes, the game just doesn't go your way. The plans you have are well-rehearsed, and your execution is down pat, but you still go for runs. This outcome is something you can't control, just like in 2000, when I was unceremoniously shat on the forehead by a giant seagull at Mannofield Oval in Aberdeen while playing for my club, Uddingston.

It was a warm day by Scottish standards, and I had been dismissed cheaply. Soaking up a few rays seemed like a good option, so I took my shirt off and put my feet up on a wooden bench outside their clubhouse. Using my thigh pad as a pillow, I dozed off while wickets continued to tumble out in the middle. Suddenly, my senses were jolted by the loud splat of seagull faeces that landed right in the middle of my forehead.

I sat up quickly, but the sheer bulk of the bird excrement resulted in the white diarrhea dripping down my nose and onto my chin. My teammates thought it was hilarious, obviously. I was in state of shivering shock. Ever since that day, the Uddingston wicket-keeper Bryan Clarke refers to me as "sh*thead".

Don't torture yourself too much, like I often did before and after games. We can't control the uncontrollable.

HOW KYLIE MINOGUE HELPED THE AUSSIES WIN THE 1999 WORLD CUP

"By removing white noise, you're able to effectively visualise what you plan to do and what the outcome will be. This process is crucial for a fast bowler."

Music provides a calming influence before taking the field. I would always put my headphones on during the journey to a game and listen to my favourite songs.

My genre preference was rock or metal - bands such as TOOL, AC/DC and even the American thrash God's, Slayer. Yes, some will see this as an oxymoron, but I found more solace in a twisting 10-minute TOOL track than a soothing Lionel Richie ballad.

Some players like to wear headphones in the changing room to zone out, but I always wanted to hear what was going on around me - to observe, to listen and to get a general feeling of what state of mind the team was in.

When you're out on the pitch, the only available tunes are the ones that are embedded in your brain. Unfortunately, they're also the most annoying of songs, often heard on the morning radio.

When we defeated Ireland in the 2005 World Cup qualifying final in Dublin, I couldn't get the song "Can't Turn Back" by Scottish pop-rock band Speedway out of my head. My wife had given me their album, and some of the tunes were catchy enough to remember.

Somewhat surprisingly, the music helped me relax on the pitch - a respite of sorts from the pressure of the game. It was a distraction that was needed, especially when I was bowling.

Singing the song inside my head when I walked back helped to eliminate the white noise. When bowlers begin walking back to their mark, they should know the plan for their next delivery.

This is when we have to switch off.

Whether this is by chatting about last night's meal to mid-off, discussing post-match plans with mid-on or singing a tune in your head, switching off is crucial.

An International Cricket Council sports psychologist I worked with in 2007 told me an interesting story. In the 1999 World Cup final at Lords, when he was taming the Pakistan top order with his typically metronomic line and length, Glenn McGrath had a Kylie Minogue song constantly playing in his head.

This was, apparently, beneficial to his performance on the biggest cricket stage of all.

I don't know what song it was. I haven't had the chance to ask him, but I can't imagine it was "Especially for You".

By switching off between deliveries, you eliminate all the distractions. When you get to the top of your mark, switch back on - get back in your bubble - like a tennis player getting ready to serve, or a golfer taking a putt.

By removing white noise, you're able to effectively visualise what you plan to do and what the outcome will be. This process is crucial for a fast bowler.

Physical endurance is vital, but so too is mental strength and clarity.

BUY THE RIGHT FOOTWEAR AND FEEL THE IMMEDIATE BENEFIT

"A podiatrist will cost a bit, but it's worth it."

I suffered from shin splints (stress fractures in the shin bones) up until I was 30. The pain was crippling. Every step I took was like being violently kicked in the shins by a Doc Martin boot. The only solace I got was placing a bag of ice on my shins at the end of the day.

In the *You Can't Control the Uncontrollable* chapter, I wrote about the moment in 1993 when selectors chose me to play for New South Wales in a four-day Sheffield Shield fixture.

However, I made myself unavailable because of my shin splints. There was no way I could've survived a four-day game.

A podiatrist will cost a bit, but it's worth it. Repeatedly slamming your feet down on the ground, with a destructive force, puts an unthinkable strain on nearly every joint in your body.

We're familiar with the pain after we bowl a few overs at the start of the season, because the next day, every part of your body aches.

But you don't have to suffer. A podiatrist will analyse your gait and how your feet land, before developing an insole specifically tailored for you.

Pronation is when the foot flattens - it's your body's natural shock absorption mechanism. When this mechanism is repeatedly occurring, it can often lead to long-term injuries, such as shin splints, lower back pain and debilitating hip soreness.

I suffered from overpronation, where the foot dips inwards, although I had no idea until the podiatrist completed her tests.

Either way, whether you have overpronation or underpronation (outside of foot takes the impact), a podiatrist will give your arch the best support possible, often by just looking at the insole of the shoe you've been wearing.

Now, 22 years later, I still wear the same orthotic insoles, and I never suffered from shin splints or long-term back pain again.

If you haven't already done so, make an appointment with a podiatrist, and have your feet examined. Whatever the cost, it will be worth it.

In terms of footwear, the quality of bowling shoes on the market now is impressive. Modern boots that are tailored for quicks are lightweight and well-cushioned, yet they still offer plenty of support.

My brand of choice was ASICS, not because it was deemed to be 'fashionable' for cricketers to wear them, but because they were the brand that suited the shape of my feet.

I have a wide foot, and the ASICS was comfortable and light. I tried other major brands, but they were too narrow a fit for me.

However, I never actually purchased an out and out, specifically designed cricket shoe.

From around 2000, I bought lighter ASICS cross-trainers for bowling, ones that had plenty of support.

Then, I would get them resoled and spiked by a company in Brisbane called Fast Bowlers United. Former Queensland fast bowlers Joe Dawes and Ashley Noffke ran the business. It was expensive, but worth every penny.

The shoes available nowadays are great for quicks. A high-quality boot that is comfortable and offers plenty of support, combined with custom made insoles and cushioned socks, will help you bowl faster for extended periods.

To bowl quick, you have to be balanced at the crease. Your footwear plays a massive part in that. Take time in choosing the right shoe.

According to research, your front foot can take up to ten times your body weight on impact with the crease. Look after your feet.

HOW TO GENERATE POWER AND ACCURACY WITH A STANDARD SEAM GRIP

I used the standard seam grip for around 90% of my deliveries. Throughout my career, the press generally labelled me a seamer, but I could swing the ball in the right conditions.

When using this grip, where you place your fingers is vitally important. Don't place your fingers tight together, because there's a higher chance you'll lose wrist control and power snap at your release point. There's also a higher chance the seam will move off the perpendicular, sacrificing accuracy, as well as potential movement off the pitch. There should be a gap of about a centimetre between your gripping two fingers, the forefinger and the middle finger.

The best way to test this is to get someone to roll a ball at you. Pretend that you're on the boundary and grip the ball, as you would when throwing it to a wicketkeeper 90 yards away.

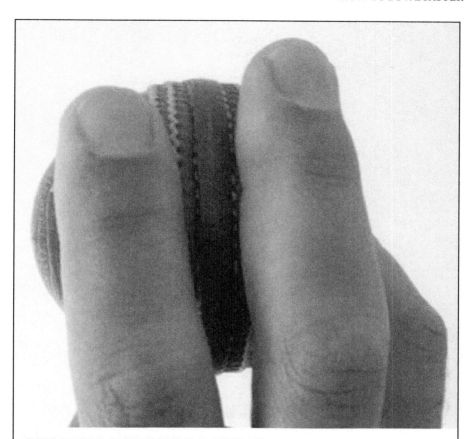

STANDARD SEAM GRIP
RELAXED GRIP WITH FINGERS SET ABOUT A CENTIMETRE APART EITHER SIDE OF THE SEAM

STANDARD SEAM GRIP FRONT-ON VIEW SHOWING THUMB AND RING FINGER POSITION

Before release, have a look at the positioning of your thumb and your two gripping fingers. You'll notice that to get ultimate power and accuracy, your two fingers are slightly parted, with a relaxed grip.

If you were to throw the ball back with your two gripping fingers close together, you wouldn't be able to generate the same amount of power.

Your ring finger rests gently on the side of the ball - helping balance your wrist at the point of release.

This natural grip works the same when you're bowling, allowing you to get maximum power and control.

If you don't apply this grip, change it now. You will increase your pace and accuracy because of it.

An important point to remember - the ball should not be deep in the pocket between your thumb and forefinger. If the ball is deep in your pocket, your wrist cannot relax, and you will lose power.

In 1994, I was coaching some youngsters at a clinic in Sydney. One boy was struggling with his accuracy, so I asked him to show me his grip.

The ball was too far back in his fingers, and his two gripping fingers looked as though they had been joined by superglue.

I showed him the correct grip for a standard seam delivery, and the benefits in accuracy and pace were immediate.

STANDARD SEAM GRIP
SIDE-ON VIEW OF THE
RELAXED GRIP WITH THE
BALL NOT TOO FAR BACK
IN THE POCKET

THE OUTSWINGER

The outswinger is a genuine wicket-taking ball, especially to top-order batsmen. However, the ball should be bowled at a fuller length, to allow the ball to swing.

At release, the seam will point toward first slip. Your fingers should remain in the same position they were for the standard seam grip, but when you release the ball, your wrist position follows the direction of the seam.

To get your wrist in the correct position, follow the rule: pinky in front of the forefinger.

It doesn't mean the ball will go to first slip, because your bowling arm is still powering down in the direction of your target. It's your wrist position that will help the ball swing, as well as releasing it with the shiny side on the right (leg-side).

For an outswinger, your target is the leg to middle stump. Don't make the mistake of trying to aim outside leg stump.

This strategy will often result in 'pushing' the ball, instead of allowing your release and follow through to flow naturally.

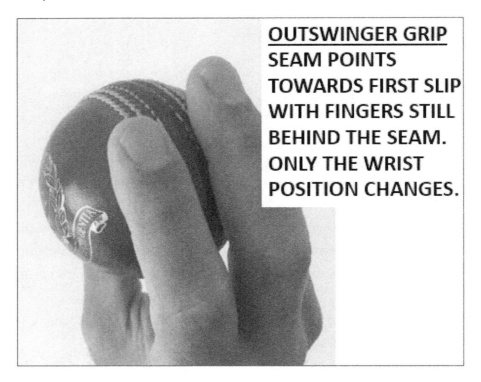

OUTSWINGER GRIP
SEAM POINTS
TOWARDS FIRST SLIP
WITH FINGERS STILL
BEHIND THE SEAM.
ONLY THE WRIST
POSITION CHANGES.

There are some factors to take into account to enable the ball to swing. Typically, there must be some humidity in the air. An assisting breeze is also beneficial.

Your release point can be slightly off the perpendicular - more 'round arm' than straight up and down.

Also, it's vitally important to ensure your bowling arm follows through, with power, down past the left side of your body. You have to complete your action, including your follow-through, to bowl an effective outswinger.

One little nuance that helped me bowl an outswinger was how I held the ball.

My finger positioning was as it should be, but there was a subtle difference. Before release - more specifically during the 'lock and load' - I would place my forefinger and middle finger on the ball's underside, rather than on top

For some reason and to this day, I can't explain why, when my arm came over, and my wrist snapped back into position, I would bowl the perfect outswinger in the right conditions.

Try it. You might get the same results, and there's no sacrificing any pace.

FINGERS UNDER THE SEAM
TRY THIS DURING YOUR DELIVERY STRIDE. IT COULD ASSIST WITH WRIST SNAPPING INTO POSITION FOR AN OUTSWINGER.

THE INSWINGER

To bowl an inswinger, the seam, and your wrist at release should be pointing in the direction of fine leg.

Your wrist position for an inswinger should follow the rule: *forefinger in front of pinky.*

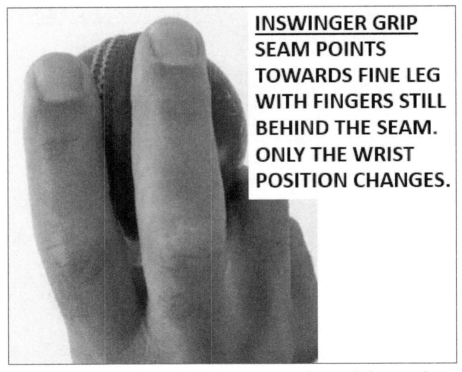

INSWINGER GRIP
SEAM POINTS
TOWARDS FINE LEG
WITH FINGERS STILL
BEHIND THE SEAM.
ONLY THE WRIST
POSITION CHANGES.

The release point should be high, as opposed to a slight round arm release for an outswinger, while the shiny side of the ball is on the left.

Secondly, your bowling arm should follow through into your body (like Jasprit Bumrah), or very tight down your left side. A wider release point at the crease is also advisable.

Some coaches advise that the bowling arm should follow through inside your body for an inswinger. If possible, try it, but it felt very alien to me as if I was bowling with a new action.

It's very difficult to complete your action if your bowling arm doesn't come down past the left side of your body in your follow-through.

If you're going against what your body's telling you, you'll lose pace and risk injury. The key to an inswinger is seam and wrist position, and a high, vertical release point.

Don't sacrifice pace. You'll take more wickets if you swing the ball at high speed.

When I bowled the outswinger, my gripping fingers were under the ball before release. However, with the inswinger, my fingers were on top of the ball. Again, without any logical reason, this helped me bring the ball back into the batsman.

FINGERS ON TOP OF THE SEAM TRY THIS DURING YOUR DELIVERY STRIDE. IT COULD ASSIST WITH WRIST SNAPPING INTO POSITION FOR AN INSWINGER.

The condition of the ball will play a significant part in whether you can make the ball talk mid-air.

I've been able to swing it both ways, with no change of action or seam direction. This movement is due to the condition of the ball, where one side is shiny, and the other side is rough.

You can employ the correct grip for outswingers and inswingers, but if the tool you're working with is substandard, you won't get the job done. Shine your ball vigorously on one side, using sweat or saliva - virus permitting.

Give yourself the best possible chance to swing the ball.

THE LEG-CUTTER

I'll let you in on a secret. Fast bowlers don't deliberately bowl leg-cutters at full speed - the grip for a leg-cutter doesn't allow it.

When I was in the New South Wales Sheffield Shield squad during the 1993/94 season, I listened in to a conversation at training between Wayne Holdsworth (former New South Wales and Australian quick) and another fast bowler.

Wayne was doing his best to convince the protege that if a speedster bowls a leg-cutter, it's not intentional. It's merely a case of the ball landing on the seam and deviating away - assuming it's a right-hand batsman.

I agree. If fast bowlers knew how to bowl leg-cutters at will, they'd be bowling them every ball.

Imagine having the ability to pitch in line with leg to middle stump, then to miraculously jag the ball away and hit the top of off stump - every delivery.

When I was a boy, commentators often praised Dennis Lillee's leg-cutter.

But, was it delivered on purpose? No.

If it were, he would've been unplayable. Even the 'Master Blaster' Vivian Richards probably would've struggled to get bat on ball against the great man.

Dennis Lillee delivered the ball with a perfect seam position and hit the pitch hard. He gave the ball every chance to move off the pitch.

When the stitching hits the pitch at above 80mph, you give yourself every opportunity of the ball deviating one way or another.

An alternative name for this grip should be "the attempted leg-cutter slower ball grip". The forefinger should rest just off the seam, while the middle finger remains in the centre.

At the point of release, the forefinger will automatically slide down the side of the ball, resulting in the seam spinning, much like a leg break.

You'll lose up to a yard of pace doing this because both fingers are not directly behind the seam, which helps to generate maximum force.

While this leg-cutter grip does sacrifice speed, if practised enough, it's an effective variation of a slower ball that can be used against attacking batsmen.

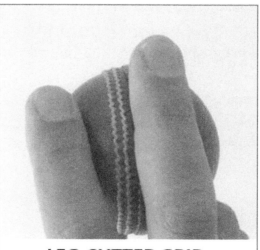

**LEG-CUTTER GRIP
FOREFINGER RESTS OFF THE
SEAM AND WILL
NATURALLY SLIDE DOWN AT
RELEASE.**

THE OFF-CUTTER

Everything I've said about the leg-cutter - apply it to the off-cutter. Just reverse the positions of your gripping fingers.

The off-cutter grip is probably the most popular grip for a slower ball because the only finger directly behind the seam is your forefinger, which lacks the power of your middle digit.

Your middle finger rests just off the right side of the seam and acts as the rudder, directing the ball to fizz like an off-break.

Again, you'll lose pace because of this, so it's another grip option when bowling to attacking batsmen.

I've hit many batsmen in the inner thigh with off-cutters. However, they're not pre-planned off-cutters - it's termed natural seam variation.

As long as you apply the correct standard seam grip, you should hit the seam nearly every ball. By doing this, you'll give yourself the best possible chance of bowling either a leg or off-cutter at full speed.

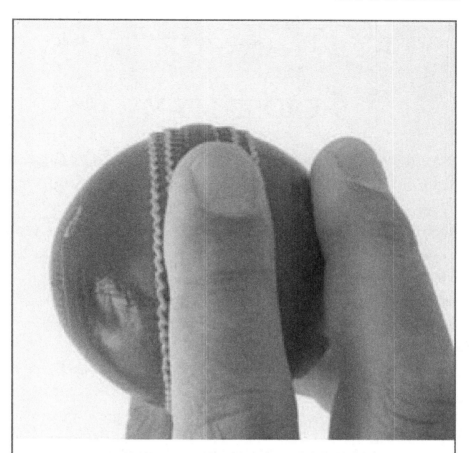

OFF-CUTTER GRIP
MIDDLE FINGER RESTS
OFF THE SEAM AND WILL
NATURALLY SLIDE DOWN
AT RELEASE.

CROSS-SEAM

The cross-seam grip should only be used when the conditions suit, or for bowling bouncers. This grip will take the shine off the ball quickly, so if you want to soften the ball, it's the best option.

But, while the seam is hard, I would always recommend using this to your advantage by 'hitting the deck' hard and giving the ball a chance to move off the surface.

Teams playing in the sub-continent will often use the cross-seam grip to rough the ball up quickly, which helps for turn and reverse swing.

The cross-seam grip works best on pitches that are dry and 'exploding' through the top. It also works on overly soft pitches.

In these conditions, if you manage to land the ball with the seam horizontal to the surface, you increase your chances of making the ball 'pop' from a length. If the ball doesn't hit the seam, then it will skid on a bit quicker.

In 2004, I was playing for Scotland against the USA in Dubai.

The pitch was dry, and after a few deliveries, I changed to the cross-seam grip, and the ball began to misbehave.

The conditions weren't conducive to swing, so it was the ideal opportunity to experiment with this grip. Nearly all of my deliveries on that day were released with the cross-seam grip because batsmen were finding it difficult to get used to the variable bounce. Play smart - use conditions to your advantage.

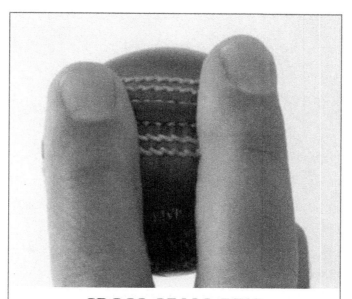

CROSS-SEAM GRIP
FINGERS REST ACROSS THE
SEAM TO GENERATE
INCONSISTENT BOUNCE AND TO
ROUGH UP THE SEAM

SLOWER BALL VARIATIONS

There are many variations of the slower ball and there's no doubting the importance of a slower ball in modern-day cricket. Changes of pace can be minor or significant, depending on the type of grip you choose.

An option is to maintain the standard seam position, with your forefinger and middle finger slightly parted on the seam.

However, the ball will be set back, deep into the pocket between your thumb and forefinger. The ball will naturally come out slower during release.

Ben Laughlin uses this grip quite often, and he rips the fingers down as if he's bowling a fast off-break.

The other variations of the slower ball have been outlined in the leg-cutter and off-cutter grips.

The only difference is that to take more pace off the ball, move your forefinger (leg-cutter) or middle finger (off-cutter) further down the side of the ball.

By doing this, *only* the finger positioned on the seam will be able to generate force behind the ball, resulting in substantial loss of pace.

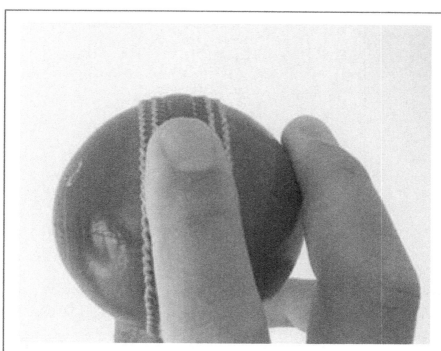

OFF-CUTTER SLOWER BALL GRIP
MIDDLE FINGER RESTS FURTHER
DOWN ON THE SIDE OF THE BALL

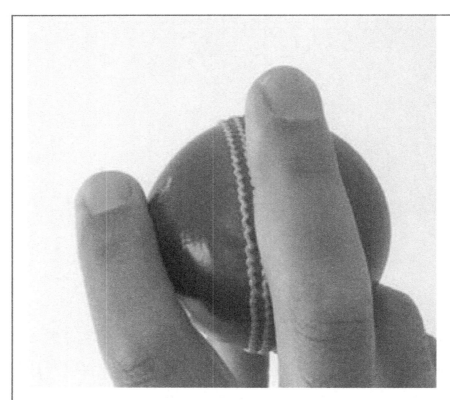

LEG-CUTTER SLOWER BALL GRIP
FOREFINGER RESTS FURTHER
DOWN ON THE SIDE OF THE BALL

The other grip you could experiment with is the split-finger grip. Craig McDermott used this grip occasionally, supposedly picked up from baseball pitchers.

I found this grip more challenging to master.

With the two gripping fingers spread wide apart, it was very challenging to maintain control at the release point. Still, it has worked effectively for others.

SPLIT FINGER SLOWER BALL GRIP
GRIPPING FINGERS POSITIONED
WIDE APART OFF THE SEAM

Possibly the most awkward grip to use for a slower ball is out the back of the hand, like a googly.

Ian Harvey, the former Australian one-day specialist, was brilliant at using this slower ball, as is Harry Gurney, the English left-arm seamer.

It's almost as if you need to be double-jointed at the wrist to execute this version of the slower ball. I experimented with this grip a lot in my twenties.

Sometimes it worked, other times it didn't.

I BOWLED AN ABSOLUTE 'PIE' TO SHANE WATSON IN THE 2007 WORLD CUP

"The boundaries were also tiny, so there was zero margin for error."

I attempted a back of the hand slower ball against Shane Watson in our 2007 World Cup fixture at Warner Park in St Kitts.

I had nothing to lose because it was my final over, and Australia were around 320.

My figures up until the last over were tidy enough: 1-40 off nine overs. I planned to starve the Aussie batsmen of any width and to vary my length.

The pitch was slow and low, which was expected because there wasn't a blade of grass on it. The boundaries were also tiny, so there was zero margin for error.

In the final few overs, Shane Watson and tailender Brad Hogg went on the attack.

Hogg's onslaught surprised me. I thought he was a bunny, but he swung the blade and connected.

I went for a couple of boundaries early in my final over. After getting slapped by Watson to the cover boundary from a yorker-length ball outside off stump, I decided that my next delivery would be a back of the hand slower ball.

Unfortunately, the execution was dire, but thankfully, the result was better.

The ball stuck in my hand, and I ended up bowling an unintentional short-pitched back of the hand slower ball.

48.4   1   Hoffmann to Watson, 1 run
Banged in short and outside off, tapped in the air towards thirdman region

48.3   4   Hoffmann to Watson, FOUR runs
Wallop! Overpitched outside off and Watson goes over extra cover.

Cricinfo commentary in my final over against Australia in the 2007 World Cup at St Kitts. It was anything but 'banged' into the pitch - it rolled out about 60mph.

"The most important skill in the execution of a slower ball is that there should be no change in arm speed."

Watson, probably more in shock than anything else, stroked it gently down to third man.

I wasn't brave enough to try it again, but I should have. It proved that a short-pitched slower ball is one of the more effective deliveries at an attacking batsman.

My final figures were 1-57 off 10. Decent enough, but going for 17 runs in my 10th over was gut-wrenching.

The most important skill in the execution of a slower ball is that there should be no change in arm speed. Slower ball grips require a lot of refining.

Try them all in training.

You may find that one or two will work better for you. In this era of T20 domination, a slower ball is a necessary part of a fast bowler's armour.

Remember, there's no point bowling a slower ball if you're not good at it. As with any skill in life, mastering a good slower ball requires a great deal of time and effort in practice.

Bowling to Australia in the 2007 World Cup in St Kitts
(Image courtesy of Hamish Blair)

GETTING THE BALL TO REVERSE SWING

"Yasir had a classic side-on, slightly slingy action which was perfect for reverse swing execution."

If you're a senior bowler who struggles to bowl above 80mph (130kph), then you might want to skip this chapter. To bowl reverse swing, you have to bowl with pace.

The Pakistani great, Safraz Nawaz discovered reverse swing by accident back in the late 70s. Now, it's a potent weapon.

Look at how Simon Jones and Andrew Flintoff tormented the Australian batsmen in the 2005 Ashes.

Waqar Younis and Wasim Akram were lethal with reverse swing in the early to mid-90s. So, what's the secret to reverse swing? There's no secret - not anymore.

When playing for The Scottish Saltires - (circa 2004-2006) - in the English domestic limited overs competition, I was fortunate enough to open the bowling with the Pakistan T20 specialist Yasir Arafat. We formed a good partnership, as our styles complimented each other.

He was the skiddy paceman who bowled a full length, while I was the bowler who 'hit the deck' and seam it about.

Yasir was a promising young quick at this time, capable of bowling up to 90mph, but he had already developed a lethal wicket-taking reverse inswinging yorker at the 'death'.

He was more effective in the final overs because of this. Yasir had a classic side-on, slightly slingy action which was perfect for reverse swing execution.

I was able to get some tips from Yasir, who went on to play a number of times for Pakistan as well as starring for the Perth Scorchers in the Australian Big Bash League.

"First of all, you need to have pace to reverse the ball. Your action is another key thing. If you try to bowl a bit round arm, you will be able to reverse the ball. And the most important thing is the condition of the ball. You need to look after the ball and make sure the ball is shiny from one side. The other side of the ball needs to be rough and scuffed up." Yasir Arafat.

Yasir Arafat celebrating another wicket for the Scottish Saltires in 2005.

The ball, regardless of its colour, should be roughed up on both sides. There are ways of doing this.

If the conditions aren't suitable for seam off the pitch or movement in the air, start bowling across the seam. This strategy will rough up both sides of the ball quickly, especially on an abrasive surface.

Secondly, you'll see that some fielders will throw the ball back to the wicketkeeper on the bounce, so it hits the square first and roughs the ball up. However, this is an action that deliberately alters the condition of the ball (Law 42.3), so umpires are encouraged to stop this from happening.

Once both sides of the ball are roughed up, vigorously shine one side of the ball with sweat or saliva. A rougher surface will allow more sweat and saliva to soak in, weighing the ball down on one side.

With the right bowling technique, speed and conducive pitch conditions, there will be a greater chance of reverse swing.

For a conventional outswinger, the wet, shiny side is facing the leg-side for it to swing away. However, for reverse swing, the opposite happens.

Even though the shiny side is facing the leg-side, the ball should tail back into the batsmen. Importantly though, the dry side has to be as rough as possible, allowing the physics of reverse swing to take effect.

Like Yasir said, bowling with a slightly round-arm action, like Shoaib Akhtar and Waqar Younis, can help to tail the ball back in, but it's not essential.

Flintoff, Jones, McGrath and Akram didn't have slingy actions, but they were masterful in the skill of reverse swing with an older ball. When you're playing on a barren pitch with no assistance, reverse swing should be your best friend.

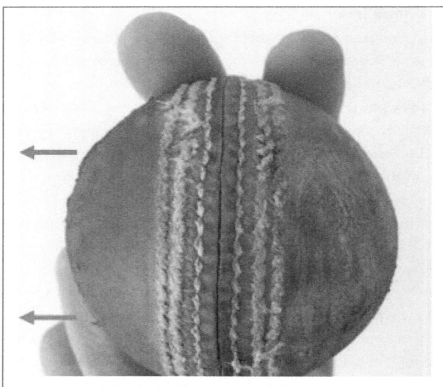

REVERSE INSWING GRIP
- **ROUGH SIDE ON OFF SIDE**
- **WET SIDE ON LEG SIDE**
    BALL WILL REVERSE INTO A
    RIGHT-HANDED BATSMAN.

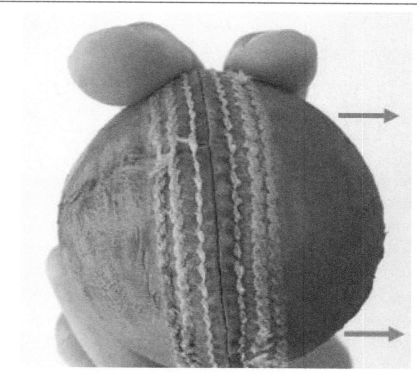

REVERSE OUTSWING GRIP
- ROUGH SIDE ON LEG SIDE
- WET SIDE ON OFF SIDE

BALL WILL REVERSE <u>AWAY</u> FROM
A RIGHT-HANDED BATSMAN.

HOW DO I DETERMINE THE LENGTH OF MY RUN-UP?

The length of your run-up depends on two things: how much of an athlete you are and how physically fit you are.

The best approaches to the crease have always been achieved by natural athletes, men who could probably run the 100 metres in under 11 seconds.

Michael Holding, Wes Hall, Malcolm Marshall, Dennis Lillee, Brett Lee, Waqar Younis, John Blain, Nick Derbyshire and Shoaib Akhtar were all great athletes. These men could naturally bowl fast, and their smooth yet brisk approach helped them gain an extra yard.

If you're unable to run the 100-metre sprint in less than 12 seconds, then it's more than likely you're not a natural athlete, but more of a cart-horse blessed with power and stamina that could go all day.

Admittedly, I was a cart-horse. I could never run the 100-metre dash in under 13 seconds.

Think of legendary fast bowlers like Darren Gough, Courtney Walsh, Geoff Tucker, Wasim Akram and more recently, Jasprit Bumrah. These were the skipper's 'go-to' men, big-hearted competitors who could bowl fast all day off a relatively short run-up.

I fell under this category. In my prime, I could bowl just as quick off five yards as I could off 20. But if I did that for too long, my body would have failed and my bowling career would have been cut short. My run-up was just 18 steps from the bowling crease. I needed it to be that long to give me enough forward momentum at the point of release.

Any shorter, I would have put my joints under too much stress, trying to gather maximum power at the crease to help compensate for the lack of momentum.

In one televised game for Scotland against Nottinghamshire, I bowled off 12 steps, because I had worked on this approach at training.

After the game finished, I took a call from my former Manly Warringah Cricket Club teammate Nick Derbyshire. He commented that I was striving too hard at the crease and that my action didn't flow as it normally did. It was one of my worst spells in a Scotland shirt.

At the start of Jason Gillespie's career with Australia, he had a very long run-up.

> *"...I felt that my run-up was too long, but my ego wasn't allowing me to shorten it. I thought, 'I'm a fast bowler, I've got to steam in from the 30-yard circle'. But it wasn't efficient. I had a couple of conversations with Greg Chappell, who was coach of South Australia at the time and decided to shorten it a little bit. Instead of coming in from 35 or 36 metres, it was 25 or 26 metres. I found that I could bowl with the same pace and for longer."*
> *Jason Gillespie. (Extract taken from Wisden.com)*

The best method to determine the length of your run-up is simple. Before practice, go to the outfield, or anywhere where there's space. Even a gym hall would do.

Get someone to wait where you think your front foot will land. Then, go back to where you feel the top of your mark would be.

Close your eyes and run through your action, as if you're playing in a game. There are no half measures here - do the drill with match intensity.

Each time, get the person to mark where your front foot lands. After a dozen attempts, your front foot should be landing in the same area.

From that landing point, use a tape measure, jot down the length and measure the distance of your run-up in steps. I used to take standard walking steps, whereas other bowlers preferred long strides. Use whatever works for you.

"I guarantee that 9 out of 10 young quicks have a different take-off point every ball."

Have another couple of run-throughs until you're comfortable with your approach.

In a game situation, use a tape measure if you can, otherwise step it out from the bowling crease.

When standing at mid-off, I often watch bowlers from the top of their mark. I guarantee that 9 out of 10 young quicks have a different take-off point every ball. They have a small disc to mark their run-up, but to be honest, on the majority of occasions the mark is pointless. Sometimes the right foot hits the mark. The next ball it's the left foot. Other times the right foot will land over the mark, but the next time, it lands just before the mark. This constant brain fog is why no balls are bowled.

Always start your take-off on the same mark. It's a simple task that, for whatever reason, gets forgotten about in a game.

A run-up is quite a delicate balance. If your approach is too slow, you put too much strain on yourself in the delivery stride. If it's too fast, then you risk losing balance at the crease, resulting in inconsistent accuracy.

Find that perfect speed where you feel comfortable as you approach the leap. Ideally, you're looking for about 70-80% sprinting capacity. What you can do, and I've done this - is ask someone to time your run-up.

When you find the perfect run-up speed, find out how many seconds it took you from the top of your mark to the release point (this was an idea given to me by the late Bob Woolmer when he spent some time with the Scotland team in 2003). Then repeat over again.

Keep practising your run up until you achieve at least a dozen deliveries near the same number of seconds. Get your body familiar with your optimum approach speed, so it becomes second nature in a game.

Throughout most of my career, I had the same run-up. When I was younger, I would sometimes go back to the 30-yard circle, because I naively thought the longer the run-up, the quicker I'd be, and the more scared the batsmen would be. Unfortunately, it doesn't work like that.

GETTING TOLD OFF BY SIR VIVIAN RICHARDS, AND FAST BOWLING FRAUDSTERS AT THE GABBA

"I assumed these 'tearaways' from Brisbane would put me to shame."

In November 1988, I was participating in a fast bowling contest at the Gabba in Brisbane during the lunch break of the first test between Australia and the West Indies.

A few regional fast bowlers, myself included, were invited to this contest against the quickest bowlers from Brisbane. The Gabba was packed.

I didn't expect to do that well. I was brisk by Rockhampton standards, but I assumed these 'tearaways' from Brisbane would put me to shame.

Aside from experience, my aim of this outing was to get a carton of beer signed by the West Indian team.

My brother was living in Brisbane at the time, sharing a house with a few lager-loving louts. For whatever reason, they wanted the West Indians to sign the carton - not the Aussies.

Anyhow, when I walked out to the middle of the Gabba during the lunch break, the pacemen from Brisbane ominously began marking their run-ups - a long way back - within touching distance of the sight screen.

As I waited at the top of my run-up, I remember one of the players saying that none of us would beat Michael Kasprowicz, who had clocked up 135kph in an earlier test.

Kasprowicz was unable to attend this event, but officials had already pencilled him in for the national final in February, 1990. That fired me up. Michael and I represented the Queensland schoolboys' team in 1988, and I didn't believe he was any quicker than me.

But here I was, stepping out of my modest run-up that had connotations of gentle medium-pace, while the Brisbane speedsters were pushing off from the distant advertising boards.

I honestly felt like I was going to embarrass myself in front of the massive crowd. I couldn't have been more wrong.

These so-called fast bowlers were genuine frauds. None of them reached over 135kmh!

My winning speed was 139kmh, (a speed that I repeated in the national final 16 months later), from an approach less than half the distance of these tall, fearsome looking, city slicker 'quicks'.

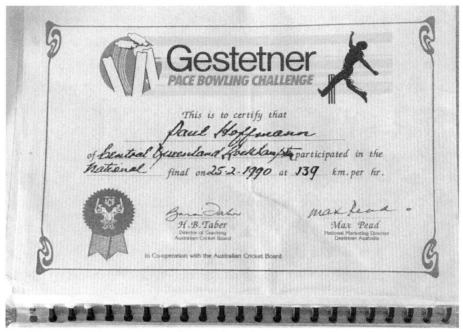

**The certificate from the national 'Pace Bowling Challenge'
final in 1990. This was held during the lunch break
of an ODI between Australia and Pakistan.**

It was a shootout where each contestant bowled three balls. As I walked off the Gabba outfield, grinning from ear to ear, my first thought was to phone my dad in Rockhampton to tell him the good news.

But before that, I made a beeline for the West Indies changing room to get my brothers beer carton signed.

At the old Gabba, the changing rooms were situated directly behind the sight screens. I walked in, stood next to the great Curtly Ambrose by the entrance. Shaking like a leaf on a tree, I asked:

> *"Excuse me Curtly, can you please sign this beer
> carton and pass it around to your teammates?".*

He then turned to Viv Richards and muttered something. Viv walked over to me, stepping over the carpet of kit bags.

I wanted to shake his hand and tell him how much I loved watching him bat and that after Dennis Lillee, he was my favourite ever cricketer.

Viv stood next to me and uttered the words I've never forgotten:

"Please leave. If you want something speak to our manager".

I was slightly disappointed that my brother wouldn't get his signed carton. Actually, on reflection, I didn't care at all.

I had just won the title of "Queensland's fastest bowler" at the age of 18, and I was about to make the call to dad that would make him the proudest dad in the state! Later on, my mum told me, (in secret until now), that dad had tears of joy when he took the call that day.

That November day at the Gabba proved beyond doubt that for cart-horses like me, a long run-up is a waste of energy. Save the long run-ups for the Brett Lee's of this world.

Sometimes, a shorter run will give you more energy at the crease, and on a flat pitch, we need to conjure up energy from somewhere.

A shorter approach could be the answer at times because conditions allow it to be.

If you discover that you can bowl just as quick off an 18-yard approach instead of 24, without sacrificing momentum, then why not change it?

You'll save yourself leg miles and be able to bowl longer spells if required.

And in case you're wondering, I didn't win the national pace bowling final. I was beaten by Warwick Adlam from Sydney. The speeds were measured by a speed gun held by an official standing behind the stumps at the bowlers' end.

CHATS WITH CRAIG MCDERMOTT, AND FINDING YOUR PERFECT APPROACH TO THE CREASE

There are not too many fast bowlers nowadays with angled run-ups like Merv Hughes, or Craig McDermott used to. Later in his career, West Indian legend Malcolm Marshall also had an angled approach to the crease.

However, Marshall was one of a kind - no bowling coach would ever tinker with his approach to the crease. His results spoke for themselves.

In 1990, I played one game with former Australian opening bowler Craig McDermott at Harrup Park in Mackay, Queensland. We were playing for Rockhampton against Mackay in a regional representative fixture. Allan Border was playing for Mackay.

As a young quick wanting to learn more, I recall asking McDermott about his angled run-up.

"McDermott said to me that the angled approach helped him to get more side-on at the crease."

When McDermott burst onto the scene in the mid-1980s, he had a straightforward and direct approach to the crease and a very high non-bowling arm at his release point. He also bowled outswingers regularly with the new ball.

But, after a spell on the sidelines between 1988 and 1991 due to injury, McDermott tinkered with his approach and action.

Like a sponge, I absorbed everything he told me. McDermott said to me that the angled approach helped him to get more side-on at the crease. It made sense. I could see what he meant.

But, as fast bowling techniques and drills become driven toward a more momentum focused and 'straight-line' approach, McDermott's side-on theory goes against modern methods.

The man known as 'Billy the Kid' had a terrific run-up, as smooth and athletic as any quick that has played the game. However, his follow-through ends abruptly.

A couple of steps after release, McDermott's momentum comes to a halt. Why? It's more than possible that because of his new angled approach, he was fighting his own body after the delivery.

With the angle of his approach, his left leg and natural momentum are heading towards the direction of fine leg as he begins the leap into his action.

Then, after release, he has to fight against the momentum of his body to get off the pitch's danger zone. Subsequently, his follow-through comes up short, and he probably lost about half a yard of pace because of this.

For someone like McDermott, who probably bowled between 135-140kmh, another yard of pace would have been lethal.

Compare this with the modern era of quicks: Brett Lee, Dale Steyn, Shoaib Akhtar, Jason Gillespie, James Anderson, Stuart Broad, Mohammad Shami, to name a few. They all have one thing in common. Their approach to the crease is relatively straight. All their energy is channelled in a straight line towards their target, adding speed to their delivery.

If you're coming in from an angle, you are then counteracting your body's natural momentum. The result? A loss of pace and more susceptibility to injury, particularly in the lower back and hip.

> *"Sometimes an action has deep-rooted flaws, and some players will find it difficult to change."*

When I worked with Dennis Lillee in 1994, I had the same issue McDermott had. My left leg was pointing towards fine leg in my delivery stride.

Before being sidelined with a severe back injury, Lillee himself had suffered from this fault.

Correcting this was quite simple, but it required a little getting used to. Sometimes an action has deep-rooted flaws, and some players will find it difficult to change.

I had to bring my front leg up in a straight line. To help achieve this, my non-bowling arm had to open up more, and my approach had to be more direct.

My non-bowling arm and front leg had to work together. Once I corrected this, I felt comfortable and was able to generate more power at the crease, as well as increasing to the length of my follow-through.

If you're struggling to run in from a straightforward approach, then, by all means, start from an angle.

However, as you reach the last eight or so strides to the crease, your approach should be straighter as you build that momentum towards the target.

A freeze frame of Dennis Lillee in 1976 before his back injury. Notice how his front foot is pointing to fine leg? His body is fighting itself at delivery.

(Image courtesy of robelinda2 on youtube.com)

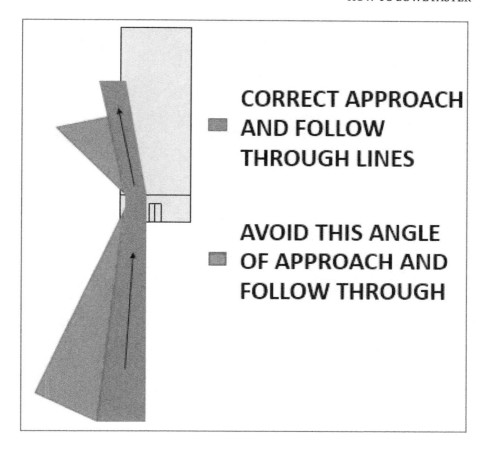

CORRECT APPROACH AND FOLLOW THROUGH LINES

AVOID THIS ANGLE OF APPROACH AND FOLLOW THROUGH

Your approach should be your natural running action. There should be no arms flinging wildly from side to side, or arms staying relatively still. The arms are used to help you gain that momentum to the crease.

Mitchell Johnson fixed his run-up by jogging the streets of Perth with a cricket ball in his bowling hand. The approach to the crease should feel as natural as possible.

FOLLOW THROUGH
MY EX MANLY (SYDNEY) TEAMMATE NICK DERBYSHIRE (FORMER LANCASHIRE QUICK) DEMONSTRATES A POWERFUL YET BALANCED FOLLOW THROUGH AT MANLY OVAL IN 1995.

I worked with a young quick last year at the request of his father. He had lost confidence and was struggling to find any consistency in his bowling. I watched him bowl a few deliveries, and it was clear what the problem was.

> *"With a new straightened approach
> and a more energetic run-up,
> his pace and accuracy improved
> tenfold within a few deliveries."*

His angled approach worked against him. He had a natural slingy action, but absolutely no balance at the crease. He casually jogged in, from an angle, before trying to launch the ball as quickly as he could toward the target. A lot of stress was being placed unnecessarily on his body.

I asked him to straighten his run-up and to speed up his approach to the crease. With a new straightened approach and a more energetic run-up, his pace and accuracy improved tenfold within a few deliveries. He was an athlete, yet he was shunning the physical attributes he had because previous mentors had not properly coached him.

As Bob Cottom (former English bowling coach) once told me that a boxer's most lethal weapon is a straight right cross. It's a fast, powerful punch thrown from a short distance in a straight line.

A fast bowler's technical mindset should follow the same philosophy. Your approach should be in a straight line, and your follow-through should carry the force of your momentum. When Channel 9 interviewed Jason Gillespie after a day's play at the Gabba, the commentator questioned him about his rhythm and why he was performing so well.

A freeze frame of a prime Michael Holding. Compared to Lillee, Holding's front foot is pointing down the pitch. All his momentum is directed towards the target - Holding was rarely injured.

(Image courtesy of M Leonard on youtube.com)

When Channel 9 interviewed Jason Gillespie after a day's play at the Gabba, the commentator questioned him about his rhythm and why he was performing so well.

His reply was simple: keep everything in straight lines, from the run-up, the pumping of the arms, the legs during delivery and the follow-through.

Bob Woolmer once told me that a fast bowler's follow-through should feel as though they're running down steps, not up them.

Don't halt your momentum. If you do, you're robbing yourself of pace.

GET YOUR LIMBS WORKING IN UNISON

Your approach to the crease will be smooth, balanced and quick enough to generate powerful momentum in the delivery stride. But your delivery stride and action are crucial - crucial for speed, accuracy and injury prevention.

Firstly, get someone to video your action. Have a look at your back foot. This step is vital because it determines where your front arm should go.

Some bowlers are classically side-on - Waqar Younis and Jeff Thomson, for example. Their back foot is parallel with the back crease, then the top half of your body should be side-on too.

In your leap, you will be looking over your front shoulder towards the direction of your target. It's important to remember that to generate momentum and pace; body parts have to be working in unison. I've touched on this in the previous chapter, particularly your non-bowling arm and front leg.

FOCUS ON THE TARGET
NIALL ALEXANDER, A YOUNG SCOTTISH QUICK, IS WELL BALANCED IN HIS LEAP, WITH HIS HEAD STILL AND EYES FIRMLY FOCUSED ON HIS TARGET.

FOLLOW THROUGH
NIALL POWERS ON DURING HIS FOLLOW THROUGH, WITH HIS BOWLING ARM BRUSHING DOWN PAST HIS LEFT SIDE, WHILE HIS EYES REMAIN FOCUSED ON THE TARGET.

(Niall Alexander images courtesy of David Potter)

If your top half is front-on and your back foot is parallel to the crease, your body will be battling a mixed action as you strive to generate pace.

On the flip side, if your back foot is pointing toward fine leg, then the majority of your top half should be front-on.

In your leap for a front-on action, you should be looking at your target from the inside of your front shoulder.

> *"If your front foot isn't pointing*
> *down the line of the pitch,*
> *it will act as a break in your*
> *momentum, slowing you down."*

Just as importantly, your front foot should always be pointing in a straight line down the pitch, not towards the slips or fine leg. Refer to the image of Michael Holding in the previous chapter.

If your front foot isn't pointing down the line of the pitch, it will act as a break in your momentum, slowing you down.

This technical flaw will result in your body 'twisting', putting additional pressure on your back and hips, making it a challenge to achieve the consistent accuracy you want. You'll also be more vulnerable to long-term injury. Refer to the image of Dennis Lillee in the previous chapter.

My back foot always pointed in the direction of leg slip. The back foot acts as a rudder, so the top half of my body followed this towards the target.

Occasionally, when I wanted to bowl outswingers or generate reverse swing at the death, I would conjure up my best Waqar Younis approach and adjust to a more side-on action. The ball was then delivered from a 'round arm' release point.

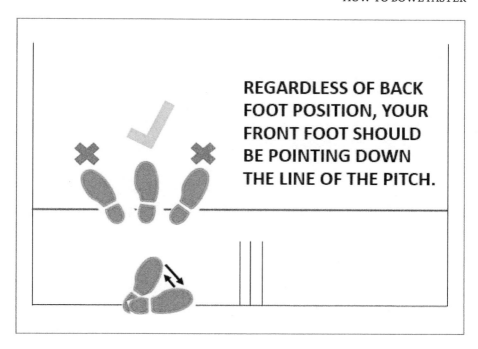

REGARDLESS OF BACK FOOT POSITION, YOUR FRONT FOOT SHOULD BE POINTING DOWN THE LINE OF THE PITCH.

"Remember, a natural action is deep-rooted, and depending on the severity of your bowling mechanics, it may take longer to adjust to any changes."

If you're worried that you have mixed action, where your top half is fighting against your back foot, then you have the option of going back to the drawing board.

This remedial tinkering is what I did after working with Lillee. Years leading up to my meeting with the great man, I struggled with back injuries because of how my front leg counteracted the forward momentum of my body.

What's the drawing board?

Break your action down in baby steps and bowl into a net, which will be no more than a few metres in front of you, ensuring that your body parts are working in unison.

For me, it was straightening the front leg during delivery, and making sure my front arm went directly up, rather than across my body.

Step through your action initially - don't jog or run. Focus on your back foot and the top half, and pull down on your follow-through. Repeat this process as many times as you can. Get your body used to the dynamics of your action.

Remember, a natural action is deep-rooted, and depending on the severity of your bowling mechanics, it may take longer to adjust to any changes.

The next step is to add more intensity to the drill, jog into your delivery stride and repeat the above process. Train your body to work with the action and build muscle memory through repetition. A change in action must be a slow and deliberate transition.

> *"His action then became so mechanical and forced that he lost pace and confidence."*

I've seen young fast bowlers suffer irreversible damage when coaches have made adjustments to their action. Yet, rather than taking cautious steps and processes to make the adjustments, these youngsters have tried to change it from a full run-up in the nets.

Some natural actions shouldn't be touched.

For example, I played with an all-rounder in Rockhampton by the name of Tim Loague. Tim had a unique skip in his delivery stride, but he bowled with decent pace and accuracy.

Then, during an off-season, he tried to change it by eliminating his 'skip'. His action then became so mechanical and forced that he lost pace and confidence. Tim then focused solely on his batting and gave up bowling.

Fast bowlers should make any adjustments with the advice and support of a qualified bowling coach.

The balance is often finding out whether a change in action is physically possible. Is your body able to cope with the adjustment?

Continuing with an action that requires some modification may be the more comfortable decision in the short-term, but in the long-term, there is only so much punishment your body can take before it breaks down.

Take time to retrain your body. Retrain it, so the action flows in straight lines, and all body parts are working in unison towards the target. Stay patient, but keep at it.

SIDE ON ACTION
BACK FOOT
PARALLEL TO THE
BOWLING CREASE
WITH FRONT
FOOT POINTING
DOWN THE PITCH.

FRONT ON ACTION
BACK FOOT POINTING TOWARDS FINE LEG AND FRONT FOOT POINTING DOWN THE PITCH.

MIXED ACTION
BACK FOOT
PARALLEL TO
BOWLING CREASE
BUT TOP HALF
TWISTS TO FRONT
ON POSITION,
RESULTING IN
GREATER CHANCE
OF INJURY.

MIXED ACTION
BACK FOOT POINTING TO FINE LEG, BUT TOP HALF TWISTS TO SIDE ON POSITION.

FIXING A COLLAPSED BACK LEG

"I view the back leg as your body's suspension mechanism. There has to be some give as your foot slams into the surface."

One of the most common faults I've seen in young quicks is that they fall away at the crease because their back leg collapses significantly. When this happens, the rest of your body follows, and you fall away. The result is a reduction of pace and inconsistent accuracy.

Some slight collapsing of the back leg is often ok because it probably feels natural. I view the back leg as your body's suspension mechanism. There has to be some give as your foot slams into the surface. However, when the collapse is quite pronounced, there will be issues.

"A back leg will more than likely collapse if the muscles in your leg and core aren't strong enough to support your body weight."

**The back leg has to collapse to some degree, because
it acts as a shock absorber.**

There are a couple of ways to correct a collapsing back leg.

Firstly, assess the speed of your approach to the crease. A faster approach run to the crease will result in greater stress being placed on your front and back foot on impact, increasing the risk of your base collapsing.

To help counteract this impact, you should ensure that your core and leg strength (particularly your quadriceps) can withstand the forces placed on your limbs during fast bowling.

Also, reassess your approach velocity. There is an optimum approach speed that will help you deliver the ball in a controlled and efficient manner.

*"...bowlers with a shorter delivery
stride tend to spend less time
on the back foot as they flow*

through the crease."

Secondly, the higher your bound and the longer your delivery stride is, your legs will naturally flex. The quickest bowlers of recent years, Shaun Tait, Brett Lee and Shoaib Akhtar had long delivery strides. Because of their core and leg strength, their legs flexed rather than collapsed, although when Tait struggled with pace and form his action fell away significantly.

Bowlers with a shorter delivery stride, such as Glenn McGrath, are less prone to their back leg collapsing. As well as that, bowlers with a shorter delivery stride tend to spend less time on the back foot as they flow through the crease.

I had a short delivery stride because my action was front-on. There was a degree of flex in my back leg, which was natural. A shorter delivery stride with a small amount of back leg flex allowed me to deliver the ball from a great height which helped me to hit the seam more consistently.

Strength and stability exercises such as squats, leg press, pull-ups and planks are essential for all fast bowlers. In chapters later in the book, I write about specific drills and activities that will help.

One of activities is to balance your back leg on a wobble cushion. When you're balancing your back leg, the rest of your body should mimic your delivery stride. The front leg should be in the air, parallel to the ground.

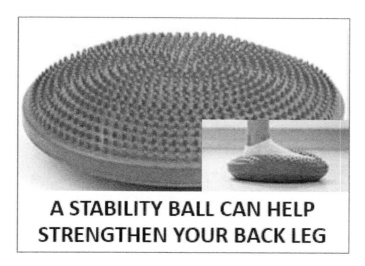

A STABILITY BALL CAN HELP STRENGTHEN YOUR BACK LEG

HOW TO PREVENT FALLING OVER AT DELIVERY

There's no doubt having a strong core, and excellent leg strength can help a bowler maintain balance at delivery. If you pause most fast bowlers at their release, there is a natural element of falling away.

There has to be to allow your release point to be as perpendicular as possible, which will improve your chances of moving the ball off the seam.

If your coach tells you that you fall away during delivery, take it on board, but ask yourself:

a) are you suffering from injury, or a lack of consistency when trying to hit your areas?
b) are you falling away drastically, to the point where you have little control of your accuracy?

If the answer is 'no', then I would be hesitant to adjust anything drastically. As I have mentioned in the previous chapter, a deep-rooted organic action is tough to amend.

> *"...if you fall away too much, you will sacrifice pace and bounce. Not only that, but you also leave*

yourself vulnerable to injury,
especially in the lower back."

Get someone to video your action, if you're falling away a little, yet you're happy with your rhythm, and you're generating decent pace and bounce, stick with it. There's no need to tinker too much with something that isn't broken.

However, if you fall away too much, you will sacrifice pace and bounce. Not only that, but you also leave yourself vulnerable to injury, especially in the lower back.

So, how do we correct an action that falls away at delivery?

Firstly, is your core and leg strength sufficient to keep you stable at the crease? I often found that young quicks, especially youths in their early teens, fell away because their muscles weren't developed or strong enough to maintain an upright position.

If you're unable to reach at least three minutes doing a plank, then your core strength has to improve. In terms of leg strength, if your back leg is collapsing, the body will typically follow. Your legs are your base - they have to be strong. I spoke about this in the previous chapter.

Secondly, are your feet aligned at the crease? If not, then there's more chance you will fall away.

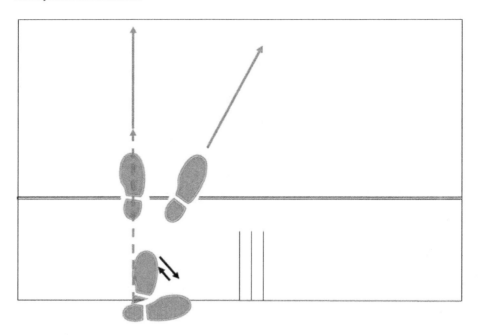

The straight line follows the correct feet alignment towards the target, which will help prevent 'falling away' at the crease. The angled arrow highlights incorrect alignment. From this alignment, the bowler's top half would have to fall away to get the ball to an off stump line.

"Many technical flaws can be solved through the correct feet alignment."

In this image, you can see that the front leg is facing the direction of fine leg, while the bowler is striving to redirect his momentum towards the target.

When you assess your video, have a look at your feet alignment. When working with young quicks at the Grange Academy, one of the first technical cues coaching director John Blain refers to is their feet positioning at the crease.

Any remedial changes to an action have to be drip fed.

Feet positioning for a fast bowler is crucial. Many technical flaws can be solved through the correct feet alignment. If your feet are not aligned, try to remedy this through a step by step process. Any remedial changes to an action have to be drip fed.

Thirdly, step through your action from the 'load' position through to the release. In the 'load' position, keep your head as upright as possible to help maintain balance.

Then, when your bowling arm goes back after the 'load', imagine that this arm is grabbing the sight screen behind you.

It might sound like a weird thought process, but remember, everything should be working in straight lines, including your arms.

As you bring your arm over to release, try to maintain an upright head position as much as possible. Your head will naturally tilt away a little to help your bowling arm remain as high as possible at the release point. Just don't allow it to fall away too dramatically because your torso will follow.

Finally, work on this with specific drills during training. Put a tramline of cones at least six metres from the crease through to the release point (refer to the image on the next page).

There should be a gap width of about half a metre between the tramline. Run through the tramline until you release the ball.

Try to keep your body and limbs working within the width of the tramline. Imagine that the tramlines are walls and you're not allowed to touch either side of the wall.

This drill, combined with excellent core and leg strength, correct feet alignment, a more upright head position at release and limbs that work in straight lines will help prevent falling over during delivery.

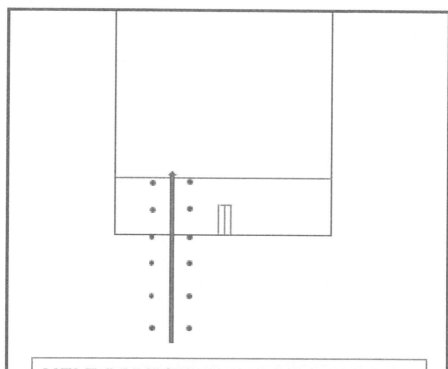

HELP MAINTAIN BALANCE AT THE CREASE BY STAYING WITHIN THE LINES BEFORE YOUR APPROACH AND DURING YOUR DELIVERY STRIDE.

An example of how you can apply a drill to help prevent falling away in an action.

(Image courtesy of researchgate.net)

One of my favourite coaches to work with was Bob Cottam, the former England fast bowler. Bob was also the England fast bowling coach between 1998-2001. As well as that, he was the assistant coach of Scotland in 2005, when we booked our place in the 2007 ICC World Cup after defeating Ireland in the final of the qualifying tournament.

England cricket legend Bob Cottam: one of my favourite coaches.

"The great fast bowlers have certain things in common. Firstly, their head doesn't fall away. If that falls away, the body will follow. Keep your head as straight as possible, and focus on your target. Secondly, their back leg powers through after delivery. If your head remains as upright as possible, then the rest of your body, including the back leg, will power through and momentum will be behind the ball towards your target." Bob Cottom,

former England bowler and bowling coach.

DRILLS TO IMPROVE YOUR ACCURACY

"I would spend hours, before and after school, bowling at a target on the side of the brick house."

Accuracy is improved by two key things: your action and practice drills. Unless you're balanced at the crease, with your top and bottom half working harmoniously together, your accuracy will be inconsistent.

Balance depends on your approach, technique and execution, as well as core strength and leg stability. As a fast bowler, my two strengths were accuracy and the ability to hit the seam consistently.

My accuracy was honed growing up in the family backyard in Rockhampton. I would spend hours, before and after school, bowling at a target on the side of the brick house, mimicking the actions of quicks from the '70s and early '80s.

The radar became robotic because I repeated the process thousands of times. As an adult, I only used one drill if I was training alone. Firstly, I would stand at the crease as if I was batting.

Secondly, I would then mark out a rectangle (two feet across and five feet long) with some chalk paint (or cones) where a good line and length was.

A good length is where it's difficult for a batsman to either drive or pull. A good line was from middle stump through to approximately sixth stump outside off.

Finally, I would set myself a goal of how many times I could land the ball in that rectangle. I would start with a target of three from each over. The more I trained, the higher the target would be.

However, a mistake many young fast bowlers make is that their eyes are focused on the target, rather than bowling with the same intensity as they would in a match. If you focus on the target, there is the risk of bowling within yourself and not fully completing your action. Rather than where I want the ball to land, my strategy is to focus on where I want the ball to be (line and height) when it passes the stumps at the other end.

If you use this as your guide, then you'll give yourself a better chance of hitting the target on the pitch. This drill has proved beneficial to young quicks I have coached.

"...when you get bored of bowling line and length, go back to bowling line and length."

Focus on where you want the ball to pass the batsman, rather than the spot on the pitch.

A TIP ON FINDING THE EDGE OF THE BAT

"...I figured that I would try something different in the second innings."

Sometimes, you'll hear the saying 'too good to get a bat on it'. It can be incredibly frustrating as a fast bowler when you have a batsman constantly playing and missing. Then, you bowl a straight one, and they hit it.

I have a solution.

In 2006, I was playing at a game in Aberdeen against Namibia. I was getting agitated because I was consistently beating the outside edge, yet the batsmen were still there.

I heard my teammates encourage me: *"Too good Hoffs!"*

That's great for the ego, but it wasn't getting batsmen out. At this point in my career, my release point was close to the stumps.

So close that I occasionally rattled the stumps with my delivery hand. If your release point is close to the stumps, you give yourself a slightly better chance of getting an LBW.

The downside? If you're moving the ball off the seam, away from the batsmen, the margin of movement will be more significant.

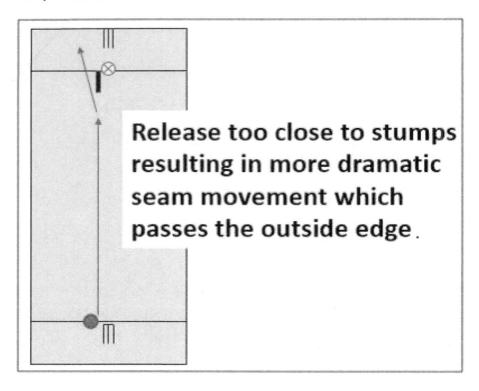

Release too close to stumps resulting in more dramatic seam movement which passes the outside edge.

After the first innings, I figured that I would try something different in the second innings - to bowl about a foot wider at the crease. My theory was that the angle created from the wider release point would reduce the margin of movement off the seam.

Firstly, the batsman would play down the line. However, because of the angle, the ball would straighten off the seam, rather than deviating dramatically. As the deviation was less dramatic, there was a better chance of finding the edge.

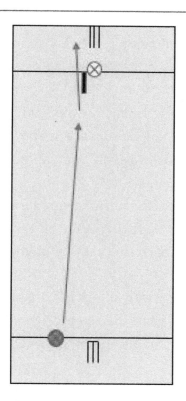

Wider release point resulting in less dramatic seam movement that catches the outside edge.

Secondly, bowling slightly wider of the crease also increased the chances of 'getting one through the gate' and bowling the batsman. As well as that, it still brings the LBW into play.

"Broad has averaged
25.71 since 2016."

Stuart Broad releases the ball wider at the crease than he used to, with impressive results. The slight angle into the batsmen makes them play more often, increasing the chances of dismissing them.

You will have heard the phrase: "make the batsman play", especially with a new ball. It's vitally important. Jasprit Bumrah creates the same angle as Broad. His statistics are also brilliant.

Fast bowling is about thinking on your feet, what can work for you in the playing conditions. Have an open mind, and don't be scared about trying different things.

According to the website cricmetric.com, between 2007-2015 (inclusive), Stuart Broad was averaging 28.83 in test cricket. Now, with a different angle of approach and release point, Broad has averaged 25.71 since 2016.

This improvement is a direct result of a more attacking line, brought about by a change in where he releases the ball. A wider release point has resulted in Broad getting more edges and more LBW's.

Stuart Broad release point comparison
(Image courtesy of youtube.com)

GENERATE MAXIMUM WRIST SNAP

The quickest bowlers have a powerful, often natural, wrist snap at their release point. Dale Steyn, Wasim Akram, Jasprit Bumrah, Andrew Flintoff and Curtly Ambrose were some examples of bowlers who could send deliveries down at around 90mph, often quicker.

When their actions are replayed in slow motion, you can clearly see their wrist snapping into place as the ball is released. Their wrist snap is natural.

But, even if you don't have the same, natural level of wrist snap, there are ways to improve on this.

The key to wrist snap is how relaxed your grip is. There can be no snap when your grip and wrist are both tense - it has to be loose.

To help with this, I leave my pinky off the ball. I also make sure the ball is not too far back in the pocket between the forefinger and thumb.

Wrist strength also helps - hand grippers are suitable for this, but I found that the wrist is strengthened when doing exercise at the gym, such as the bench press, bicep curl, tricep lifts and medicine ball throws, etc.

Some bowlers like to have their wrist cocked in position as they run in, which is fine. However, it can't remain in that position as your bowling arm rotates in your delivery stride. The wrist snap happens at the point of release.

To practice wrist snap, have a partner stand at least five metres away from you. Using power generated from only your elbow through to your fingers, throw the ball to your partner. After about ten throws, get them to stand further back.

Focus on generating power from your wrist. Your wrist should snap and release the ball, with your hand following through to the target. The seam of the ball should remain upright. Keep doing this drill and as you become stronger, keep getting your partner to stand back further.

Also, look at increasing the weight, so instead of using a ball, use a small weight sphere (like a mini medicine ball) used in fitness drills. These typically weigh about 1.5kg and can be purchased online.

A relaxed grip on the ball and a strong wrist will automatically add pace to your delivery.

The key to having good wrist snap is for your wrist to be strong,

yet relaxed when delivering the ball. Wrists are strengthened during weight lifting exercises, but a simple tool like the wrist gripper is also a handy accessory for a fast bowler to have.

(Image courtesy of physioroom.com)

TACTICS OVERVIEW

Over the next few chapters, I will be looking in detail at tactics that can be used for different types of batsmen, as well as different stages in an innings.

It has been said that that particular batsmen don't have a weakness. Wrong.

Every top-order batsman has their kryptonite, especially when they're new to the crease.

This weakness is the top of off stump, or just outside off stump at a good length (the same length practised in the accuracy drill).

Regardless of whether it's a T20, a 50 over match or a longer version of the game, your aim is to hit the deck hard on an off stump line.

Every top-class fast bowler will study batsmen, even if it's picking up trigger movements, technique (backswing and feet) as well as common scoring areas.

When I was fielding, I would always look at the feet of the batsman. I would then look at how they play certain deliveries and what areas they are looking to score.

My aim, aside from taking wickets, was to suffocate the batsman by cutting off their scoring options, through field placement and diligent bowling disciplines.

Every batsman is different, but your set-in stone tactic should be to hit the deck hard - on or just outside off stump.

"Try to hit the top of off stump or

hit them on the head - it's simple".

New Zealand speedster Lockie Ferguson with his straightforward yet effective plan in the 2019 World Cup. (Quote courtesy of telegraph.co.uk)

TACTICS FOR A BATSMAN 'PLAYING IT SAFE'

"...the objective of any bowler with a fiercely competitive mindset is to get them out."

There are methods of dealing with a 'boring' batsman - a batsman who prefers to play it safe. Some methods are more conventional than others (more about that later in this chapter).

You can have an attacking plan and use a variety of slower balls, yorkers, bouncers, wide half-volleys to test their patience, or you can keep bowling an immaculate corridor.

While a negative batsman may not score freely, the objective of any bowler with a fiercely competitive mindset is to get them out.

The longer a 'safe' batsman remains at the crease, the more comfortable they'll become, which may eventually lead to them playing some attacking shots.

THE BLOCKER
WE'VE ALL COME UP AGAINST THE BATSMAN WHO 'PLAYS IT SAFE'. BUT, RATHER THAN KEEPING THEM IN, LOOK FOR WAYS TO GET THEM OUT.

(Image courtesy of David Potter)

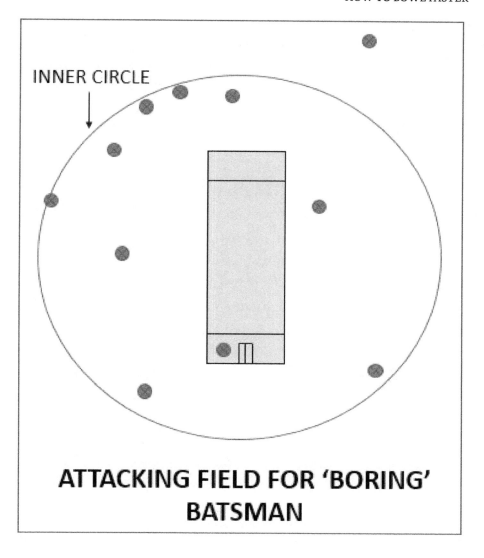

INNER CIRCLE

ATTACKING FIELD FOR 'BORING' BATSMAN

I employed a hybrid philosophy to get boring batsmen out - that is, a mixture of 'top of off' deliveries and attacking deliveries.

Set an attacking field, including a gully, a couple of slips and a short cover. Set traps and entice them into taking risks by leaving gaps in the field settings. Mix this up with some bouncers and slower balls, and bring a fielder under his nose on the leg-side. Don't be shy about coming around the wicket either.

Yes, keeping a 'boring' batsman at the crease may seem like a good idea, especially if his partners at the other end are dropping like flies. But, time and time again, I've seen these types of batsmen come out of their shell and play winning knocks. For example, their first ten runs come off an excruciatingly painful 50 balls. Then, with ten overs left in the innings, they scramble an additional 50-70 runs, while lower-order sloggers steal a few streaky boundaries.

Suddenly, the opposition total goes from 70 to a tricky 150, thanks to the resilience of the 'dull' batsman. Aim to get them out. Don't ever allow them to lull you into a false sense of complacency.

In 1999, when playing for Uddingston Cricket Club against Aberdeen, I tried an unconventional tactic against their best batsman, Neil McRae.

Not a Darren Gough-like tactic of pulling funny faces in the approach to the crease, but something much more stupid and daring.

McRae, the current head coach of Jersey cricket, was a stubborn opening bat, unflappable and fiercely determined. I wanted to do something different to put him out of "the zone".

The game was in Mannofield, Aberdeen's home ground. They had the best tea's in the league, and their doughnuts were amazing. Not only were they the size of a lawn bowls ball, but they were incredibly tasty. Our former scorer, Colin Blackwood, dared me to bowl one of the doughnuts. That sowed the seed for me. I couldn't help myself.

As we walked out to the pitch, I hid the doughnut under my sweater, nursing it carefully while I marked my run-up. I gave the actual ball to Graham Robertson, who was standing at mid-off. I had to let him in on my tactic to upset McRae. Rather than talking me out of it, he turned away and chuckled to himself.

I ran up to deliver the first 'ball' of the innings, keeping the cake tucked inside my right hand. Deliberately, I bowled a beamer to McRae, because I didn't want the doughnut to explode when it hit the pitch. It didn't make any difference. McRae ducked to avoid the beamer, but the cake exploded mid-air.

It wasn't the outcome I was expecting. The intention was to get the doughnut to my wicketkeeper, Bryan Clarke, on the full. Unfortunately, giant doughnut crumbs were now scattered the full length of the pitch.

Clarke, ever the class clown, whipped his gloves off and began to pick the scraps off the pitch, devouring them like a starving dog off the street.

After a telling off from the umpire and a quick clean-up operation, the match continued. McRae went on the make a patient half-century as Aberdeen took the spoils. The lesson here? Stick to conventional methods.

BODYLINE

Another effective strategy for a conservative batsman, or any bats-man, providing you're quick enough, and the pitch is conducive to pace and bounce, is to come around the wicket and bowl short, into the batsman's body.

Aim for the armpit, or as former Aussie quick Joe Angel once said, "hip to heart". Because of the angle, it's tough for a batsman to play a pull or hook shot, or to keep it along the ground.

Position your field accordingly, with a packed leg-side, including a leg slip or leg gully, short square leg and a silly mid-on. Have someone on the boundary at deep square. This tactic borders on 'Bodyline', and it has made a comeback of late.

The New Zealand quicks employed this short-pitched bowling tactic against Australia in their 2019 series, and it proved to be effective, even against the seemingly impenetrable Steve Smith.

Your execution of any strategy depends on one thing: your speed, skill and discipline. The rules are strict when it comes to the number of bouncers you can bowl each over, so again, it's a skill you need to practice.

If the delivery is too short, good batsmen will sway out of harm's way. If not short enough, it becomes easier to play off the back foot. This plan can work, but your execution has to be precise.

For example, it's all very well saying that you will adopt a Glenn McGrath type line and set an attacking off-side field, but you have to execute this for it to work.

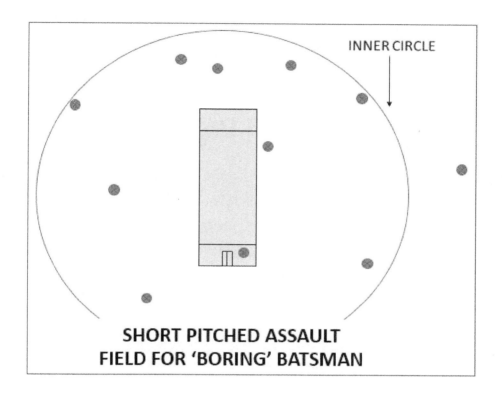

INNER CIRCLE

**SHORT PITCHED ASSAULT
FIELD FOR 'BORING' BATSMAN**

HOW TO BOWL TO AN ATTACKING BATSMAN

"...too many quicks are now running up and just hoping for the best, especially when they're 'under the pump'."

T20 cricket has changed how cricket is played. Bowler's need to think on their feet, and be quick to adapt to conditions and where batsmen are targeting them. Batsmen don't just build an innings in T20; they try to dominate the bowlers from the outset.

It never used to be like this. Bowlers used to be able to find their rhythm after a few balls, while the batsmen typically 'had a look'. Now, it's frenetic.

Even 50 over matches have evolved into an extended version of T20, with scores of 350+ becoming more frequent. Let's be honest. It's not an easy gig being a fast bowler in T20 cricket.

When T20 was in its infancy, we expected spinners to be the 'whipping boys'. Unfortunately, it's the opposite.

"The modern fast bowling cartel is becoming far too predictable, with the slower ball being one of the primary culprits."

Quick bowlers are cannon fodder for flat track bullies; pitches are flat, and boundaries are small. Bats are enormous, and field restrictions favour batsmen. Crowds want to see runs; to witness balls clearing the ropes as frequently as possible. T20 is a fast bowler's graveyard.

However, let's not throw in the towel just yet. Yes, we know we have to be smart - to be one step ahead of the batsmen.

Bowling to aggressive batsmen requires a detailed plan, but from what I've seen, too many quicks are now running up and just hoping for the best, especially when they're 'under the pump'.

Trying to contain an aggressive batsman on a flat wicket can be a nerve-wracking experience. When nerves consume your body, thinking becomes clouded and pre-match plans are often discarded completely.

Like with any important event, whether it's a job interview, a best man speech or a presentation, the more you prepare, the less anxious you will be on the big day. Bowling in a high-pressure situation is no different. Prepare, plan and practice.

The modern fast bowling cartel is becoming far too predictable, with the slower ball being one of the primary culprits.

The skill of fast bowling is being undermined with speedsters over-complicating what should be a simple plan.

There are effective tactics fast bowlers can use that will help not only contain rampaging batsmen but also to send them sulking back to the T20 dugout.

The following chapters look further into this and will provide strategies and ideas that will help you achieve better results against aggressive batsmen.

NEW BALL TACTICS TO AN ATTACKING BATSMAN

"In the Australian Big Bash League (BBL), the memo to quicks with the new ball is to hit the top of off stump."

Regardless of the format you're playing, make use of the new ball. Give the ball, irrespective of its colour, a chance to 'talk'. Your over-riding focus in your initial overs should be to hit the 'deck' hard in the 'corridor of uncertainty'. This focus has to be the plan from ball one. In the Australian Big Bash League (BBL), the memo to quicks with the new ball is to hit the top of off stump - not too full and not too short. In other words, the 'Pigeon' (Glenn McGrath) length. Hit the pitch hard and give the ball a chance to move either way off the seam. The criminal offence with a new ball is to offer width to batsmen. Alternatively, if your strength with the new ball is to move it through the air, give the ball a chance to swing.

Kyle Coetzer in action for Scotland.
(Image courtesy of Donald MacLeod donald-macleod.com)

"I found the hardest new ball bowlers to hit were those who hit the pitch hard just back of a length and were also able to nip it back." Kyle Coetzer MBE, Scotland captain and former Durham professional.

If you're bowling outswing, set a deep point or deep cover early on if you have to. Once the lacquer has gone, the white ball doesn't swing conventionally like a red ball.

Therefore, in white-ball cricket, it's a common tactic to take the shine off the ball as quickly as possible after the first ten overs.

Do this by bowling cross-seam to soften the ball, making it more challenging for batsmen to strike the ball cleanly. It also allows bowlers to work on generating reverse swing earlier than usual.

But what if you're up against skilled operators like Jonny Bairstow, or

Jos Buttler, who are teeing off from ball one on a flat track?

Do you revert to death bowling? It's definitely a viable plan, especially if the pitch is offering minimal sideways movement, but fielding restrictions make this option difficult.

In this case, your plan should be to focus on *four* primary target areas - areas that you will need to practice religiously at training, so you're able to adapt quickly when you're under pressure in a game.

"It only takes a small amount
of movement off the pitch
for the batsman to mistime
a shot and get caught."

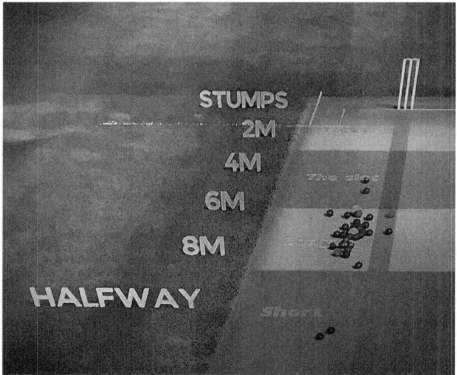

This is a pitch map of Josh Hazlewood's deliveries against

England in a 2020 ODI fixture. He only went for 26 runs off his 10 overs. Aside from the length, the key here is the lack of width offered, which is what batsmen prey on.
(Image courtesy of bbc.co.uk)

The first target is still a back of a length Josh Hazlewood type delivery that doesn't allow a hitter like Bairstow to free his arms. As Scotland captain Kyle Coetzer has said, the most difficult ball for an aggressive batsman to face with the new ball is the one that nips back off the seam.

Batsmen like Bairstow and Buttler are strong square of the wicket and are susceptible, particularly Bairstow, of getting bowled through the gate from a delivery that seams back off a good length.

Remember, the sweet spot of a cricket bat is about the size of a hand palm. It only takes a small amount of movement off the pitch for the batsman to mistime a shot and get caught.

When you're bowling the Hazlewood length, have a fielder on the deep square leg boundary.

> *"...don't discount coming around the wicket and aiming the yorker wide of off-stump."*

The *second* target is the yorker length, preferably a foot outside off stump, with a deep point or deep cover fieldsman in place.

However, it goes without saying that if you opt for a yorker length outside off with the new ball, then your execution has to be perfect. Also, don't discount coming around the wicket and aiming the yorker wide of off-stump. The angle will make the leg-side ramp almost impossible to play, and the batsman will find it more difficult to score from if you have deep cover in place.

If you opt for a deep point or deep cover fieldsman, bring third man up to the edge of the circle. Keep the fielder at deep square leg for the swipe across the line to your back of a length delivery.

Don't think of these two field placements as being defensive. If the batsman is swinging hard, then both of these fielders will also get catching opportunities.

Your *third* target is different varieties of a slower ball, simply because you don't want to become predictable. However, don't feel the need to revert to a slower ball too quickly, especially if you're not getting hit.

> *"Stay patient, stay disciplined*
> *to your plan and back the skills*
> *that you've practiced."*

Finally, try the head high bouncer outside off stump, especially on grounds with big square boundaries.

This delivery, bowled at either full or reduced pace, is difficult to keep along the ground, and it's a tactic that's becoming more widely used, both in the first powerplay and at the death.

Chris Gayle is often targeted in this area by quicks. When he played on the big Aussie stadiums in the BBL, Gayle kept skying the ball to either mid-on or mid-off because he just wasn't able to control the shot. Neither could he leave the ball - his instinct and ego told him otherwise.

For a compulsive hitter like Bairstow, this is an option - albeit risky - to add to your counter-attacking plan. Again, it brings a deep point fielder into play.

Stay patient, stay disciplined to your plan and back the skills that you've practiced.

If you're playing club cricket and using a red ball, that's a different scenario. Make the most of the new ball and keep shining it on one side.

The world's best batsmen struggle when they're facing a bowler moving the ball either in the air or off the pitch. However, if you're faced with a pinch-hitter, keep the above T20 four-point plan in mind.

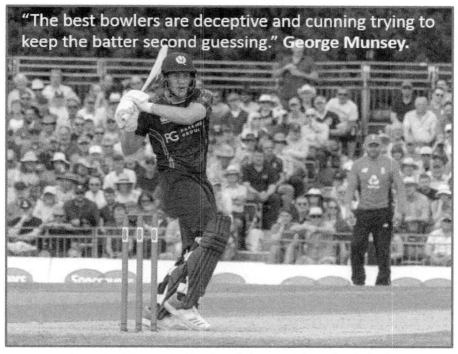

George Munsey, Scotland International, global T20 and T10 franchise player.

(Image courtesy of Donald MacLeod donald-macleod.com)

SETTING A FIELD FOR THE NEW BALL

"Always look to get wickets early. Make use of the new ball and set your field so that there are attacking catchers."

Much of this depends on the playing conditions, such as the state of the pitch, overhead conditions etc.

It also depends on the type of bowler you are, whether you're a genuine swing bowler or a 'back of a length' 80mph+ seamer.

During the initial overs of limited-overs games, you're typically allowed only two fielders outside the circle.

The question is, should you go with a 6-3 or a 5-4 field? Regardless of the format, if you're generating prodigious outswing with the new ball, common sense would favour an attacking 6-3 field.

Always look to get wickets early. Make use of the new ball and set your field so that there are attacking catchers.

The most effective way of slowing a run-rate is to take wickets.

A typical 6-3 fielding plan would include two slips, backward point, third man, cover, mid-off, fine leg, mid-wicket and mid-on.

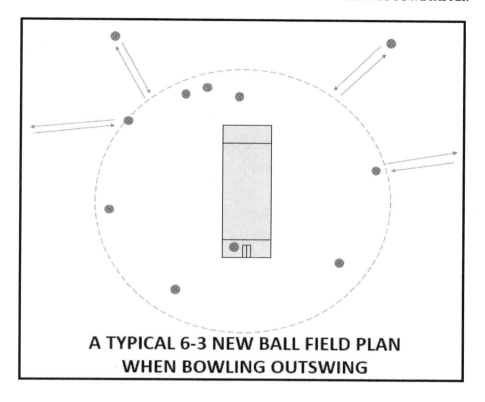

**A TYPICAL 6-3 NEW BALL FIELD PLAN
WHEN BOWLING OUTSWING**

*"The only time I would drop
square leg back early would be
on slower pitches and when
there's little or no swing."*

With outswing, you can be innovative with field placings if you back your skills. Some bowlers prefer to bring fine leg up to the inner circle and drop the square leg back.

This tactic depends on your plan. If there's pace in the pitch and you intend to bowl a bouncer or two with the new ball, then a fine leg is a better catching option.

A fine leg also covers any inside edges or tucks off middle stump when you target the LBW or bowled dismissals with a straighter delivery.

The only time I would drop square leg back early would be on slower pitches and when there's little or no swing.

The number of slips you have depends on the movement you're generating. I wouldn't go for any more than two slips in the initial overs, especially if there's little assistance from the pitch. I've often favoured one wide first slip with a gully and point, with a third man to sweep.

A risky option with the new ball would be to bring third man up to the circle and drop point back to the boundary. If you're bowling a fuller length, then this could be a viable option. Both the short third man and deep point then become catching options.

> *"If the pitch is offering generous pace and bounce, keep your fine leg back because glances off the bat will be finer when there's more speed on the delivery."*

However, if you're aiming to bowl a consistent 'top of off stump' line, as I normally did, go with a 5-4 field.

This standard field would include a wide slip, point, third man, cover, mid-off, mid-on, mid-wicket, square leg and fine leg.

Again, depending on the length you want to bowl, you have the option of bringing fine leg up on the circle and dropping square leg back.

If the pitch is offering generous pace and bounce, keep your fine leg back because glances off the bat will be finer when there's more speed on the delivery.

Although, on a slow pitch that is not conducive to short pitched bowling, a deep square leg is both a run-saving and a wicket-taking option.

Opening batsmen who go hard at the ball on a sluggish surface will favour the 'cow corner' arc, dragging the ball between deep mid-on and deep square leg.

I often went with this new ball plan, especially against batsmen like Matt Prior, who loved to hit across the line early on, often going aerial. Having a fielder in the deep, just forward of square, will help suffocate that option, especially when you're bowling a tight line on or just outside off stump.

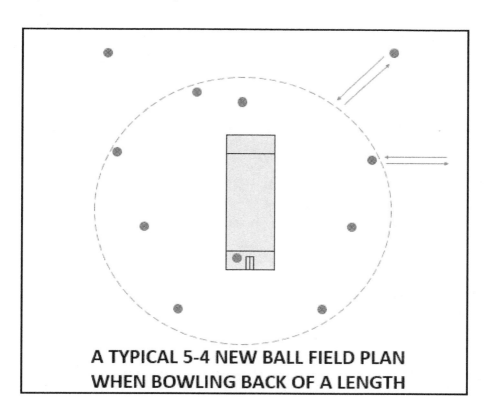

A TYPICAL 5-4 NEW BALL FIELD PLAN
WHEN BOWLING BACK OF A LENGTH

Regardless of the level of cricket, we should always have a plan for an attacking batsman.

DEATH BOWLING

"...they're bowling poorly executed random deliveries that are cannon fodder for quality batsmen."

In this chapter, I have gathered comments and thoughts from current and former first-class cricketers, batsmen who have faced the finest bowling attacks in the world. I wanted to find out what batsmen DON'T want when they're batting in the final overs.

From watching a lot of cricket over the past decade, it appears that nowadays, many quicks are guilty of experimenting with 'funky' variations when bowling at the death, or when bowling to a batsman who's dominating at any stage of the innings.

Deliveries are saturated with a concoction of slower balls, bouncers, attempted yorkers, low full tosses, high full tosses. It's as if they're bowling without a clear plan, possibly as a result of muddled thinking driven by anxiety.

Or, the plan they had didn't work, so they're bowling poorly executed random deliveries that are cannon fodder for quality batsmen. There's no plan 'B'. These bowlers end up confusing themselves.

"...he has a simple plan, and he honours that plan religiously."

The best death bowlers can remain composed in the heat of the battle, with the tenacity and skill to be able to execute and to stick to a plan, with field settings set accordingly.

Effective death or powerplay bowlers keep it very simple because they can execute their skills on command.

One of the most effective death bowlers in the world right now is Jasprit Bumrah, because that's what he does; he has a simple plan, and he honours that plan religiously. He doesn't overbowl the slower ball and his go-to delivery is the low full toss or yorker.

Scotland international Calum MacLeod, who belted a quality England attack for an unbeaten 140 off just 94 balls in 2017, has had plenty of experience batting in the final overs.

MacLeod is a 360-degree batsman, a skilful, wristy player with the ability to hit straight and ramp the quickest of bowlers.

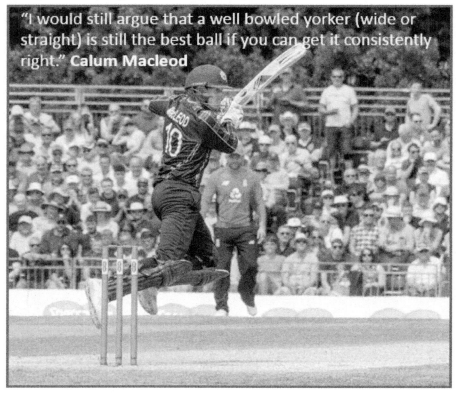

"I would still argue that a well bowled yorker (wide or straight) is still the best ball if you can get it consistently right." **Calum Macleod**

Calum MacLeod, Scotland International, former Warwickshire and Durham cricketer.

(Image courtesy of Donald MacLeod donald-macleod.com)

"I would still argue that a well-bowled yorker (wide or straight) is still the best ball if you can get it consistently right. The best bowlers tend to mix it up a bit more than just sticking to one ball, making it harder to get set and guess what they are about to bowl. With field settings, I think it's important that the bowler has a couple of options of what they can bowl - try to make the batsman hit over or past the boundary fielders." Calum MacLeod, Scottish International.

The often undervalued yorker. When executed it remains a very difficult ball to score from.

As a fast bowler, you have to visualise yourself as an attacking batsman, facing you. Where do you NOT want the bowler to bowl?

When I opened the batting for my club and Scotland, my role was to 'whooshka' as many boundaries as possible, while the fielding restrictions were in place.

I prayed on length and width, but when you aim to belt boundaries, there are certain areas where you don't want the bowler bowling to you.

The first is a full yorker or low full toss, on the stumps. Batsmen can't hit perfectly placed yorkers for six, and it's very difficult to hit them for four.

The second is a wide full-length delivery outside off stump, especially when there's a fielder at deep point or cover. That limits a batsman's scoring option.

Ed Cowan, the former Australian test batsman, Scottish Saltires and Sydney Sixers star, made it clear what the majority of batsmen don't want when they're facing quicks in the final overs.

> *"The most difficult ball for a batsman to face at the death is a wide yorker, with a third man and deep point. If executed, it's hard to hit a six! Batsmen can maybe only deflect past keeper for four or carve past point." Ed Cowan, former Australia, New South Wales and Uddingston opening batsman.*

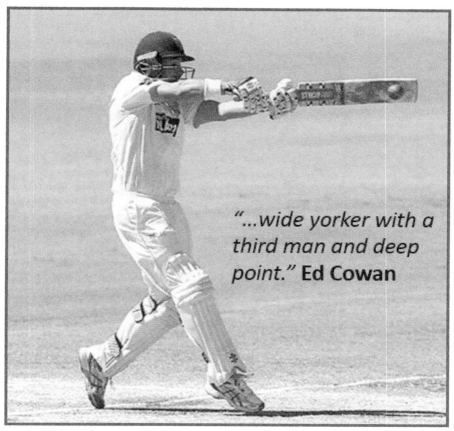

"...wide yorker with a third man and deep point." **Ed Cowan**

Ed Cowan in full flight for New South Wales.
(Image courtesy of Ed Cowan)

A wide yorker is an excellent tactic, but, as Ed commented, this all depends on your execution under pressure.

Zimbabwe all-rounder Sikandar Raza was named the 'Player of the Tournament' in the 2018 ICC World Cup Qualifier, thanks mainly to his batting prowess in the death overs as his economical off-spin.

**The wide off stump yorker, as shown here, is difficult
to hit for any batsman in attacking mode.**

I first played against Sikandar in Scotland and he impressed me greatly with his ability to improvise and find gaps in the field. He was also capable of brutal hitting when required.

Sikandar echoed the thoughts of MacLeod and Cowan regarding effective bowling final over bowling plans.

*"The yorker is going out of fashion a little, but
it is still the most effective ball at the death
and the most difficult to score from, because
it's very difficult to scoop." Sikandar Raza.*

Sikandar Raza, Zimbabwe all-rounder and specialist finisher.
(Image courtesy of cricket365.com)

When you attend training, repeat drills that help nail your wide yorker. If you regularly practice bowling yorkers at batsmen who are treating their last six balls as a T20' bash-fest', then your execution will undoubtedly improve in a game situation.

Remember, repetitive drills lead to muscle memory, making game execution better.

When a batsman is giving you the classic Dean Jones 'charge', where should you bowl to them?

> *"...batsmen who charge are looking for width to free their arms."*

Firstly, you can stick to the yorker plan, but, remember too, that batsmen who charge are looking for width to free their arms.

If you fall short on your wide off stump yorker and the batsman has given you the charge - or even if they've remained in an orthodox stance, don't be surprised if you get drilled over the mid-off or cover boundary.

The best option for a charging batsman is to deprive them of width. Bowl into their body and tuck their arms up, or bowl a straight yorker. It's very difficult for a batsman on the move to effectively drive straight down the ground.

I used to charge a lot in my pinch-hitting role, and I would always preempt where I wanted the ball to be delivered.

An off-side length ball outside the line of your body is what charging batsmen want. Avoid that.

Your kryptonite to a charging batsman is to either bowl a wide or straight yorker or hit the deck hard, aiming for the hip-heart area.

Slower balls are very effective, but only if the execution is perfect and not too predictable. Gavin Hamilton, a star performer in the 1999 World Cup, is one batsman who found a short slower ball tough to hit at the death.

Every batsman has different strengths. What may work for one batsman may not work for another. Despite it being overused at times, a slower ball remains a crucial skill for bowlers to have.

Don't, however, feel as though you have to bowl slower balls, simply because it's T20 or limited-overs cricket. It's a mistake substituting pace and skill with ineffective slower balls.

Also, most modern batsmen have become wise to changes of pace.

When I played in the 2007 World Cup, our analyst found that the Aussie batsman hit approximately 67% of their boundaries off attempted slower balls.

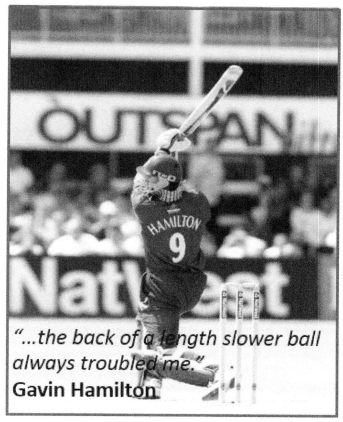

"...the back of a length slower ball always troubled me."
Gavin Hamilton

**Gavin Hamilton, former Yorkshire, Scotland
and England all-rounder.**
(Image courtesy of Donald MacLeod
donald-macleod.com)

I bowled that one slower ball to Shane Watson in the final over. I didn't need to change it up. The Warner Park straight boundaries were small, and the wicket was flat. My objective was to keep a tight line and hit back of a length, preventing batsmen from hitting down the ground.

Yes, use slower balls if you're good at bowling them, like Ben Laughlin or Harry Gurney. But, don't become predictable.

"...a well-executed wide or straight yorker remains the most effective delivery at the 'death'."

Remember, for the majority of batsmen, a well-executed wide or straight yorker remains the most effective delivery at the 'death'.

If batsmen can improvise and hit wide yorkers for boundaries, even with a field that has been set for that delivery, then sometimes you have to applaud their skill. With respect, not many club cricketers can do this.

In terms of bowling to 360-degree batsmen who can target every boundary, don't become predictable. But at the same time, don't over complicate matters.

In the *"New Ball Tactics to an Attacking Batsman"* chapter, I wrote about a four-target plan to a batsman like Jonny Bairstow. Revert to this plan at the death.

Without giving width, aim for back of a length deliveries. Make the batsman hit across the line towards deep square leg and change your grip for subtle variation to your speed. This can be particularly effective, especially on a sluggish pitch. Also, vary your release points for example, deliver from wide or close to the stumps, or bowl the ball from 24 yards.

When bowling to a 360-degree batsman at the 'death', I would favour the wide off stump yorker (possibly delivered from around the wicket) and have a deep mid-off and a deep cover in place.

Finally, use your slower ball options (including the slow bouncer), which have already been outlined in previous chapters.

If you can execute your skills down pat, then setting a field becomes much more manageable. 'Death' bowling is all about damage limitation. Wickets will come because batsmen take more risks.

Trent Woodhill, the former Melbourne Stars coach and current advisor to Cricket Australia, spoke to me about plans that international fast bowlers use at the 'death' in T20 franchises around the world.

"A lot of bowlers seem to be rotating a wide yorker, leg stump yorker and an off-speed slower ball." **Trent Woodhill**

Trent Woodhill, Professional coach, T20 innovator and Cricket Australia advisor

(Image courtesy of Aaron Francis, News Corp, Australia.)

"It's now a case by case basis. With batsmen like MS Dhoni, DJ Bravo and Maxwell, stay away from wide yorkers - though to the tail it's the go-to. Bowlers seem to be rotating a wide yorker, leg stump yorker and off-speed slower ball. This last one starts being

the main go-to at the back end of tournaments when the surface is more used and slower. At the MCG we encouraged our quicks to still hit the deck at the death, as the square boundaries are so big. The target was ribcage." Trent Woodhill.

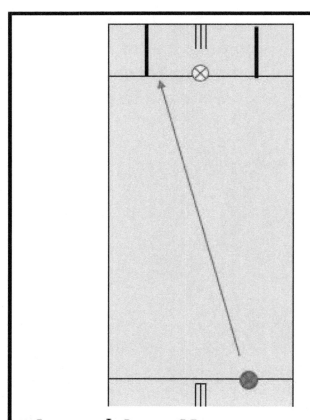

The wide off stump yorker delivered from around the wicket is a very difficult ball to score from.

SETTING A FIELD FOR DEATH BOWLING

If your plan follows the strategy that I outlined in the previous chapter, then a number of fielding positions are crucial. Remember, no more than five fielders are allowed outside the circle.

Firstly, I believe a deep square leg is crucial for straight back of a length deliveries and slower balls, where batsmen who are late on the shot will inevitably drag to deep 'cow' or square leg.

With the plan of bowling wide off stump yorkers and low full-tosses, you'll definitely need a deep point and a long-off.

That's three positions covered. The other options are either: a third man, a fine leg and a long-on.

I would be inclined to have a long on, simply because if you're bowling back of a length and the batsman comes down the pitch and drives straight, you have that scoring option covered.

Who do you bring into the circle - the fine leg or the long-on? That depends on the batsman's strength, but not many batsmen can scoop a wide off stump yorker down to fine leg.

If the majority of your deliveries are going to be wide off stump yorkers, then the changeable positions outside the circle should be the third man, fine leg and long-on. The other three positions, deep square, deep point and long-off should be set in stone.

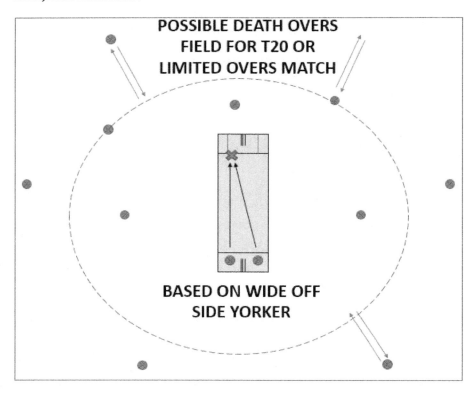

POSSIBLE DEATH OVERS FIELD FOR T20 OR LIMITED OVERS MATCH

BASED ON WIDE OFF SIDE YORKER

DEVELOP GOOD TRAINING HABITS

"...fast bowlers need to micromanage what they do."

A fast bowler's body is their temple. Look after it. Usually, club players participate in two training sessions a week. Unlike batsmen, who can belt throwdowns until the sun goes down, fast bowlers need to micromanage what they do.

If the training session goes for two hours, don't spend this time bowling. Be sensible with the number of deliveries you bowl. Look to bowl a maximum of four overs in the first hour.

The rest of your time spent in that hour should focus on either fielding drills, batting or bowling specific exercises, with a medicine ball, for example.

In the second hour, bowl another three to four overs. That's a total of 16 overs bowled during training in a week, which is more than enough. I would even suggest bowling less than that.

The problem is, in some sessions, batsmen are left without net bowlers, and you end up feeling sorry for them. That's not your problem. It is a problem for the coach who is organising the training session.

Coaching staff should not overwork fast bowlers during the week. Make it clear to them you have a limit on the number of overs you want to bowl.

Over bowling in training only leads to fatigue, which leads to injury. Don't bowl any more than four overs before having a break.

I was guilty, especially earlier in my career, of not bowling at 100% in the nets. I always held back, probably because I knew I was going to be bowling for at least an hour or so.

It wasn't until I was training for Manly Warringah Cricket Club in Sydney, when a senior player pointed out that I wasn't bowling at the same speed and intensity as I did in a game.

He was right, and it made sense. Bowling in training should always mimic what you do in a game. The intensity and effort should be just as focused.

My former Scotland coach Tony Judd wouldn't allow us to bowl a warm-up ball when net training began. Why? Because you want to train your body to bowl fast, all the time, from ball one.

Tony Judd, my former Scotland coach, never wanted the quicks to have a warm-up delivery in training.

(Image courtesy of bbc.co.uk)

Bowl four-over bursts at practice - take a rest, maybe do some fielding drills, and then bowl another few overs at match intensity.

Would Usain Bolt have jogged through his 100m sprints during training to prepare for an actual race? No.

The same applies to fast bowling. Get your body and mind used to running in and bowling quick. It then becomes routine or second-nature in a game, and you'll be capable of bowling at increased and sustainable speeds for longer periods in a game.

THE DAY OF THE MATCH

"One aspect of a pre-match warm-up that used to annoy me was the amount of time spent on fielding drills."

I'll touch on pre-match diet later in the book, but in terms of physical preparation, you must have a routine.

Begin stretching early in the day, in the shower even. After breakfast, go for a light walk or bike ride to wake the senses.

Try to have all your kit ready the evening before. We shouldn't rush preparation. Energy has to be channelled towards your performance. When you get to the ground, have a look at the approaches from both ends. Visualise yourself running up to the crease. Importantly, begin to get a feel for the dynamics of the ground.

One aspect of a pre-match warm-up that used to annoy me was the amount of time spent on fielding drills.

As a fast bowler, I wanted to get as much bowling time just off the square during the warm-ups.

I didn't want to spend 30-45 minutes doing intensive fielding drills. Fast bowlers need to get a 'feel' for the ground - we have to become familiar with approaches and get a 'feel' for the crease. Whilst the length of a pitch is 22 yards; every ground is different.

When I played at Edgbaston (in a Sky Sports televised game against Warwickshire in 2006) and The Oval (a late September fixture against Surrey in 2005), I found the creases of these test match grounds difficult to adjust to, because both creases were at a higher level to the approach.

It felt as though I had to 'jump up' to the crease, rather than being just able to 'flow' through my action. I didn't get enough warm-up time in the middle to get comfortable with the idiosyncrasies of these pitches.

It may sound selfish, but tell your coach you need at least 20 minutes of warm-up bowling time in the middle, even if it means segregating yourself from the rest of the team.

From my experience, an assistant coach or fellow player would rather take a mitt to the quicks anyway. Your teammates will want you to be 'game ready' from ball one. They won't begrudge you from skipping another 20 minutes of fielding drills.

Do what you have to do to ensure your performance is not compromised.

FITNESS

If you want to bowl fast, you have to be fit. Fast bowling is the most physically demanding role in cricket. But some specific exercises and activities will help you become a quicker and more potent bowler.

By developing specific muscle groups, you'll not only improve the power and speed required to bowl fast, but you'll also help prevent potential injury.

Repetitive drills that work your bowling muscles and closely mimic your bowling action are essential.

Drills develop muscle memory, which is what fast bowlers require to maintain a good rhythm and sustained pace.

The following chapters take a closer look at particular activities to improve bowling specific cardio fitness, as well as strength and speed drills that will undoubtedly add pace to your deliveries.

The only thing bowlers should be thinking about are our plans to batsmen and our field settings. The action of bowling should be second nature.

From the age of 40, I suffered from career-ending pain in my right shoulder. It was no coincidence that the pain began after I stopped going to the gym on a regular basis.

**Fraser Watts and I working on shoulder
strength drills in Scotland training**

The muscles around your shoulder joint have to be strong. These muscles add stability to the joint. Without that additional strength and stability, you're risking injury.

Once I returned to the gym and targeted my shoulders, the pain disappeared.

OFF-SEASON CARDIOVASCULAR FITNESS PROGRAMME (GYM MEMBERS)

Let's assume that you're a member at a gym. In the off-season, it's essential to keep your fitness levels high. If you put on weight in the off-season, there's a higher chance of sustaining an injury during the cricket season.

Bowling long, high-quality spells requires a good cardio engine. But, don't just spend hours on the treadmill each week. Your joints won't enjoy the continual pounding, even if it's on a cushioned platform.

The following programme was my typical week of cardiovascular activities at the gym.

Monday

Rowing machine - 10 x one-minute bursts at full 100% effort with 30 second rests in between each minute. Depending on your fitness levels, you could start with five bursts and work your way up to 10.

Tuesday

Treadmill. Pre-set interval training, alternating between high-intensity running and walking. Set the treadmill for 10 minutes, or more if required.

Wednesday

Cross trainer - 20 minutes of whatever programme you desire.

Thursday

Rowing machine: Aim for 5000 metres.

Friday

Five minutes on the bike and then follow with a repeat of Tuesday's treadmill programme.

This fitness programme is a guide. You can mix it up as much as you want, have a day off if need be, but it's essential to incorporate cardio into your workouts.

Better still, if you have access to a pool, use that at least twice a week - and stay away from the gym.

What distance should you swim? That depends on your ability, but I aimed for 400 metres doing freestyle.

OFF-SEASON STRENGTH PROGRAMME (GYM MEMBERS)

With the modernisation of sports training, specialist coaches are developing new techniques to help maximise aspiring fast bowlers.

However, none of the specialist techniques were any more effective than simple drills at the gym.

I worked in close unison with Andy Jackson, the former Scotland conditioning coach, on strength and fitness. Your strength programme should work in tandem with your cardio sessions.

It will also be more intense in the off-season, as you don't have the time constraints and recovery periods as you do when you're playing. My strength programme was straightforward and easy to follow. Nothing fancy, just proper old circuit training on different weight machines. The machines I used were as follows:

- Leg press
- Hamstring curl
- Lat pulldown
- Shoulder press
- Chest fly
- Bench press (free weights and bar if possible)
- Abdominal crunch/leg lifts
- Back extension

- Cable tower - attach a handle with your feet wide apart as you would in a delivery stride, and pull down with maximum power, as you would in a bowling action - use for both arms, as your non-bowling arm helps you to generate maximum pace with a fast and robust pulldown (image on the following page)

For each machine, I would do three sets, but rather than completing a set of 10, for example, each set would last 40 seconds, before a 20-second rest.

This strategy was a personal preference, so if you wish to work in sets, then go for it.

As a fast bowler, you are focusing on fast-twitch fibres when you do strength exercises.

PULLDOWNS
POSITION FEET AS IF
YOU WERE BOWLING
AND PULL DOWN
WITH BOWLING
ARM. ALTERNATE
BOTH ARMS SO YOU
ALSO WORK THE
NON-BOWLING ARM.

The quickest fast bowlers will all have excellent fast-twitch muscle fibres, whether that's natural or helped through a specific and effective strength plan.

When you do your repetitions, work your fast-twitch fibres. For example, when pushing up in the bench press or leg press, push up with power, then lower the weight gently.

By reducing the weight gently, you'll put strain on your muscles, which helps to develop strength and stability.

Your weight should be heavy enough to allow you to execute the drill effectively.

Too light, and you will push the weight up too fast. Too heavy, and you will risk injury. Find the right weight that will allow you to execute the drill with fast-twitch focused power.

How often should I attend the gym? I would advise that my suggested strength programme should be completed three times a week, to allow for recovery.

Ensure that your sessions at the gym are done at maximum output. Get your body and mindset tuned to the intensity of being a lethal fast bowler.

On your off days, continue with cardio drills or go for a swim.

OFF-SEASON CARDIOVASCULAR ACTIVITIES (NON-GYM MEMBERS)

No access to a gym or pool? Easy.

Find a park, or use your cricket outfield. Make your activity bowling specific by performing shuttle sprints. We did these when I was playing for Central Queensland, as well as Scotland. A typical shuttle sprint session is as follows.

Sprint 20 metres - walk back to start
Sprint 40 metres - walk back
Sprint 60 metres - walk back

How many repetitions of this? That depends entirely on your fitness level. Progress at a slower pace if you're not at a decent level of fitness. I would start with five sets of these and work my way up to 10 after a few months.

You could, however, keep going until you're cooked, but sets give you a target, which can be a good thing in strenuous activity, such as shuttle sprints.

Do this activity twice a week, possibly on a Tuesday and a Friday.

If you want to mix it up a little, go for a run. For example, to mimic the rigours of fast bowling, I would use street poles as a guide.

Walk between two poles (usually around 20 metres), and then sprint for the following three poles (60 metres). Repeat this as you pound the pavements in your local neighbourhood.

Interval running is perfect for fast bowlers. It mirrors the stop-start intensity of bowling in a game, and it improves your aerobic and anaerobic performance.

On the days you're not performing shuttle sprints, ride a bike, or take a walk. The key is to maintain cardio fitness during the off-season. You will reap the benefits when the season starts.

The street poles along Moss Road in Bowmore. These were a useful guide for interval running! This was where I would run during my holidays in Islay, a Southern Hebridean island off the west coast of Scotland.

(Image courtesy of Google Maps - Moss Rd, Islay, Scotland)

OFF-SEASON STRENGTH EXERCISES (NO GYM)

Invest in a barbell and weights.
(Image courtesy of unsplash.com)

Not everyone can afford the gym, but that's no excuse not to maintain strength and fitness. You can also buy a bench, a barbell with weights and use this at home, possibly if there's space in the garage. These items are cheap, yet so versatile.

The medicine ball is a great strength and fitness tool
(Image courtesy of Unsplash.com)

Regular drills with a medicine ball will help strengthen your core and stabilise muscles, as well as developing the fast-twitch muscles used in fast bowling.

A medicine ball can be used as a warm-up still before a game or training session. It should be a mandatory piece of equipment for any quick.

Here is a typical set of activities that you can do, as often as you want, during the off-season. I used to aim for a minimum of three days a week.

- Leg Squats - 3 x 10 reps with 30-second rest in between. Hold a towel above your head to maintain posture and go down so that your thighs are parallel to the floor.

- Forward Lunges - 3 x 10 reps

- Medicine ball throws - hold the medicine ball high above your head and then throw it to the ground in front of you. Try doing this with your feet placed as they would be when you're bowling. 3 x 10 reps

Medicine ball age and weight guide
10-12: 1kg
12-14: 2kg
14-17: 3kg
17+: 3-4kg

- Push-Ups - 2 x 20 reps (more if desired)

- Incline Push-Ups 2 x 20 reps

- Pull-Ups - 2 x 10 reps, using a pull-up bar (inexpensive to buy).

- Abdominal crunch or bicycle Crunch

- Forearm plank - hold for as long as possible

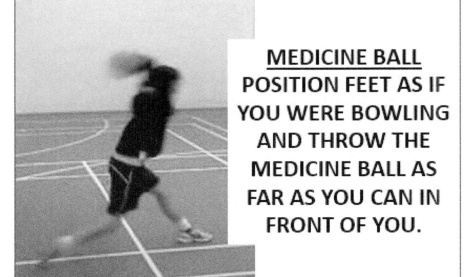

MEDICINE BALL
POSITION FEET AS IF
YOU WERE BOWLING
AND THROW THE
MEDICINE BALL AS
FAR AS YOU CAN IN
FRONT OF YOU.

(Image courtesy of Cricket Strength on youtube.com)

FITNESS ACTIVITIES DURING THE SEASON

Strength and Cardiovascular

The same off-season drills will also apply when the season starts, however, you will need to be smarter as to when you do your workouts.

Like a boxer, your fitness training should be programmed towards your maximum physical output on game day. Work your body hard earlier in the week and taper down the intensity as the match draws nearer.

For example, on a Friday, don't hammer your legs at the gym or pound away on the treadmill. Your legs need a rest before the game. If you do a leg press workout on a Friday, you'll have 'jelly' legs on a Saturday, especially after a few overs. This has happened to me before.

When you have no strength in your legs, bowling fast is impossible, because stability at the crease is compromised.

If you have played cricket on a Saturday and Sunday, then the following is an example of a strength and fitness routine for the rest of the week.

Monday (recovery)
400-metre swim or 30 minutes on a cross-trainer.

Tuesday

Follow the cardio and strength workout following programmes outlined in the previous chapters. A typical session at the gym could look like this:

- *Warm-up - active stretch routine should include hamstring scoops, walking lunge twist, arm circles, followed by five minutes on the rowing machine at medium intensity.*
- *Upper body circuits*
- *Interval training on the treadmill (high intensity for 3 minutes and low-intensity for 30-60 seconds - repeat)*
- *Leg circuits*
- *Warm down: static stretch routine should include: posterior capsule stretch, hamstring stretch, quadriceps stretch, followed by a swim or 5 -10 minutes on a cross-trainer*

Wednesday

Low-intensity swim or walk/jog or rest

Thursday

Similar to Tuesday, but mix it up a little bit. Use a cross trainer or do some skipping for a warm-up. For strength, focus on your legs first rather than the top half. As it's closer to game day, reduce your repetitions.

Friday

Rest or 400-metre swim

DIET

"I lasted five minutes in the session before vomiting and collapsing on the riverbank grass."

Fast bowlers have to be physically fit and strong. We know that because we run more and push our bodies to its limits. But optimum performance is not just about being physically and mentally fit.

What you eat in the evening and the morning of a match is vitally important. A batsman's weakness is back of a length just outside off stump. A fast bowler's weakness is food. I don't know of any quicks who didn't enjoy their food.

It was my weakness, which is why at the age of 12, I stupidly thought I could break the Guinness Book of World Records for the most number of grapes that could be eaten in five minutes.

After riding down to Vince's fruit shop in Park Avenue's Main street and collecting two kilograms of black grapes, I went home and told mum I was attempting to break a world record and that she had to adjudicate the attempt. Mum being the joyful person she was, laughed and went along with it.

After devouring close to one and a half kilograms in the allotted time, I couldn't stuff in any more grapes. Not long after, I suffered from crippling stomach cramps while my mum consoled me with a few 'I told you so's".

I was slow to learn the lesson of how bad food habits can adversely affect your performance.

I was a keen boxer in my teenage years, and in one particular training session, we had to run up and down the riverbank in Rockhampton. Just before this I gave into temptation and bought a hot dog and chocolate milkshake while in a local shopping centre. I lasted five minutes in the session before vomiting and collapsing on the riverbank grass.

"I ate 12 Weetabix at a posh hotel in Abu-Dhabi after winning the man-of-the-match award..."

In 1996, I was in Rockhampton, playing my first game for about six months after suffering from a back injury during my time as a professional cricketer at Colwyn Bay in North Wales.

The match started at midday, so about an hour before, I had two banana sandwiches and a large mug of Milo. After two overs in the Rockhampton humidity, I took a knee at fine leg, staggered off and retired myself for the day.

A few years later, as part of a job interview, I was participating in a life-saving test one morning at a pool in Hamilton, outside Glasgow. After 'rescuing' a fellow participant in the middle of the pool, I quickly began to feel nauseous and light-headed. At the advice of the examiner, I crawled to the nearby first-aid room and slumped on the physio bed. I shouldn't have demolished eight Weetabix for breakfast and needless to say; I didn't get the job.

Early one morning (before my teammates had risen) in November 2004, I ate 12 Weetabix at a posh hotel in Abu-Dhabi after winning the man-of-the-match award against Kenya the day before.

It was my way of treating myself and still remains my personal record.

There's no doubt my sugar-heavy diet of simple carbohydrates held me back at stages in my career. We often hear coaches talk about the one-percenters to improve performance.

Your overall diet adds much more than one percent. Elite sports-people are disciplined in what they eat.

For most of my time playing cricket, I worked hard on my physical fitness, but I lacked consistent discipline with my diet.

My younger sister, Elizabeth, has been a nutritionist and dietician for two decades now. In the process of writing this book, I asked for suggestions about meals for fast bowlers - foods that will contribute towards sustained performance throughout the day.

The following pages include her recommendations about what foods to eat and the best times to eat them.

Evening Before a Match

For a pre-evening match meal, something 'light' and low in fat (to aid quick digestion), but still carbohydrate-based with some protein would be best.

So, for a pre-evening match meal, her suggestions are:

- sandwiches/wraps/bagels with lean meat or spread, and fruit
- sushi rolls
- smoothies
- jacket potato with baked beans/tuna/cheese
- healthy pizza (sticking with leaner meats such as chicken or ham and smaller amounts of cheese)
- wholegrain toast with baked beans

You can have rice or tomato-based pasta dishes with some lean meat and vegetables. For example, stir-fries are a sensible option but note how you feel during play after eating this. For some, it may be too heavy and cause gut upset. For others, it may work out fine.

Pre-Match Breakfast

For breakfast, you can have a substantial meal, although this depends on your starting time.

Ideally, have breakfast four hours before a game to allow your stomach to digest it. You may then need a small carb-based snack an hour before play if required (such as fruit/yoghurt/wholegrain crackers with cheese).

Suggestions for breakfast include:

- porridge oats with low-fat milk or yoghurt, and fruit
- wholegrain toast or English muffins, with baked beans or eggs, and low-fat milk and fruit
- fruit & milk-based smoothies, e.g. banana
- fruit toast with low-fat milk or yoghurt
- Greek yoghurt with blueberries and muesli

Nutrition targeted towards your needs as a fast bowler can make a massive difference in terms of sustained output. When we stayed in motel rooms, it was difficult not to get carried away with the smorgasbord of breakfast options, especially considering it was free. I tried sticking to carbohydrate foods, such as waffles, with some scrambled eggs. If I overate, I felt heavy and sluggish. But it was such a struggle to contain myself from the mountain of food options. Every fast bowler was the same.

Also, stay clear of energy drinks before a match.

In December 2006 when on tour in Bangladesh with the Scotland team, I experimented by downing a can of energy drink before I went onto the field.

At lunch, we did a urine test to check our hydration levels. I was dehydrated, even after consuming the full contents of my water bottle during the drinks break.

Energy drinks give you a short burst, but the comedown is harsh and will be detrimental to your performance.

Two days later, I drank a water-based hydrate-fuelled mix before play. In the lunchtime urine test, my hydration levels were excellent, and I felt so much better. I had a sense that I could continue to bowl for as long as I wanted. I didn't have that feeling two days before when I just wanted to sleep.

The lesson here? Stay clear of high sugar energy drinks if you want sustained performance. If you do love an energy drink, then complement that with plenty of electrolyte-based drinks.

RESPECT THE UMPIRES

Simple manners go a long way in every walk of life, but particularly on the cricket field. Fast bowlers are a competitive lot, often fiery in temperament with a tendency to blurt out expletives at the most inappropriate moment.

Be kind to the umpire.

In a game of cricket, the umpire has to be your best mate. Most umpires will make a decision based on their judgment, but, with the close decisions, a little love might go a long way.

It could lead to you taking the match-winning wicket, an LBW decision that, if a fiery ill-tempered bowler had pleaded for, may not have been given out.

At the start of your spell, thank the umpire for taking your cap, and tell him your action. You could even engage in a little small talk, usually about the weather, or how the pitch is looking.

Most importantly, if a close appeal is turned down, don't throw the toys out of the pram - let others (usually the keeper from my experience), do that.

THE UMPIRES
THESE INDIVIDUALS SHOULD BE YOUR BEST FRIEND ON THE PITCH. ALWAYS RESPECT THEIR DECISION AND GET ON WITH IT.

Scotland umpires Billy McPate and Mac Wylie
in the 2010 Scottish Cup final
(Image courtesy of David Potter)

Stay calm and whatever you do, don't stop on the way back to your mark with a diva attitude and demand:

"What's that missing sir?"

The umpire is not obliged to tell you. Put yourself in their shoes. Would you like your decisions questioned - constantly? No.

Instead, throw a comment at the end of the over as you trudge to the wilderness of fine leg. "That LBW must have been tight, or was it a tad high?"

This way, you're not challenging the umpire. You're asking the question, but going about it in a less confrontational and condescending manner.

It's a conversation that draws out a response, and you add a possible reason as to why it wasn't out. Then you keep walking to fine leg, usually after getting the obligatory "well bowled" backside slap by one of your teammates. Treat the umpires with respect.

You cannot change a wrong decision. Get over it.

Instead, build bridges early doors. Build a positive relationship with the umpire. You may sway their mind with that faint outside edge tickle, or the 50/50 LBW shout.

This LBW appeal in the 2010 Scottish Cup final was close, but it was given not out, so I just got on with the game.

(Image courtesy of Donald MacLeod donald-macleod.com)

IGNORE THE BOUNDARY EXPERTS

*"I was on the receiving end of
a foul-mouthed tirade from
a spectator in Nairobi..."*

There's nothing more annoying than 'boundary experts' - critics that have very little or no experience at playing the game at a decent level.

I was quite fortunate that my Rockhampton upbringing gave me a thick skin. As a rookie playing against senior men in the '80's, I copped it on and off the field. Sledging was a part of the game, and no quarter was given. I once struck a tailender in the head, and he fell to the ground, holding his head. He was out of his crease at the time, so our captain quickly ran over, picked up the ball and whipped the bails off. The umpire upheld the captain's run-out appeal, while ropeable opposition players carried their wounded batsman from the pitch. That tailender was 'Jock' Carroll, my representative coach who I spoke about earlier in the book.

Nights out on the town were just as bad. The drink brought out the worst in some men, and I recall getting a 'gobful' from an opposition player about 'bowling too short too often'.

So, in 2007 in a game against Kenya, when I was on the receiving end of a foul-mouthed tirade from a spectator at the Gymkhana Ground in Nairobi, it didn't overly concern me.

"Hoffmann man you're f**king sh*t!"

"Hoffmann man I'll be waiting for you!"

"Hoffmann man I'll find out where you're staying!"

My only worry was that on the morning of this match, John Blain and I were woken by a string of phone calls to our hotel room. I answered the first call, only to have a gentleman shouting down the line, accusing me of owing him money and that because of me, he couldn't feed his family. I hung up just as he requested my credit card details, but the phone kept ringing. In the end, we pulled the socket out. Was it the same man giving me 'dog's abuse' later that day? I'll never know, because I never saw him again. Unless the advice is from someone you respect, treat criticism with a pinch of salt.

My dad was selective when to offer advice because he knew I didn't enjoy constant feedback. On one particular occasion, when playing grade cricket in Rockhampton, I was struggling with my rhythm. Afterwards, my dad told me that I had been dropping my left arm too quick in my delivery. I didn't tell him I was struggling - he knew and was able to pinpoint a minor technical issue that I could fix immediately. The 'boundary experts' are nothing more than white noise. Ignore them.

My dad was one of the few people I'd listen
to when it came to feedback.

IGNORE THE CRITICS
MOST CLUBS WILL HAVE
BOUNDARY EXPERTS WHO ARE
OFTEN OUTSPOKEN AND OVERLY
CRITICAL. STAY FOCUSED ON
WHAT YOU WANT TO ACHIEVE.

RESPECT THE GAME AND DON'T SHOULDER BARGE BATSMEN.

It's ironic that I'm writing this chapter, considering that a short video of me shoulder barging an opposing player is used as an example of a Level 3 offence in the ECB online umpiring course.

People don't remember the important wickets I took or the number of Scotland caps I achieved. They only remember my shoulder barge from 2007, which seems to have gathered a few fans on the video streaming network, youtube.com.

The usual question is: why did you do it? Now, I can finally set the record straight and answer this question.

I was on tour in Kenya with the Scotland team, playing in a tour-nament against other associate countries that would determine T20 World Cup qualification later that year. It hadn't been a particularly enjoyable tour. My camera was stolen from our changing room in Mombasa and we were mostly confined to our hotels.

I recall being quite grumpy at times, and I even gave my teammate Fraser Watts a stiff uppercut to his ribs one night when he stole some french fries off my plate without asking. Normally I'd be happy to share. There was also the phone call incident, which I write about in the *Ignore the Boundary Experts* chapter.

The shoulder barge incident happened in a game against Canada in Nairobi. The game before that, we had played Ireland at the Gymkhana ground. I had bowled a delivery to Jeremy Bray, the dashing left-handed opening batsman. He played a defensive shot to the off-side and took off for a quick single. His opening partner, William Porterfield was sprinting to get down to the strikers' end.

At one point, Porterfield was between myself and the ball. For a brief moment, I contemplated dropping the shoulder on Porterfield, so I could get to the ball. I felt as though he was preventing me from potentially running him out.

Was it intentional? I doubt it. Porterfield always played the game in the right spirit. I wasn't fully aware of the rules, but I thought a little nudge would be fair, considering my direct line to the ball was being obstructed.

In the 'shoulder barge' video on youtube, I was presented with a similar scenario against Canada. John Davison played a defensive shot towards mid-wicket. Like Porterfield, Abdool Samad was attempting to get to the strikers' end.

In the video, you can see that I was running to the ball, but in the corner of my eye, I could see Samad. If we continued, we probably would have had to side-step each other. So, in a moment of madness, I detoured off my line and dropped the shoulder on Samad, knocking him sideways.

Gary Baxter, the New Zealand umpire, gave me a telling off and said I was on report for "a deliberate use of the shoulder". John Davison, a respected Australian first-class cricketer playing for Canada, swore at me in disbelief, shouting - "you're f**king kidding!".

When I took my fielding position down at fine leg, Don Maxwell, the Canadian all-rounder, began calling me "John Cena". His fellow teammates didn't find it funny.

I regretted the incident immediately. Samad was a classy batsman and I apologised to him after the game, which we won in the final over.

I attended a hearing with the match referee shortly after, and pleaded guilty to the offence. I was fined 50% of my match fee, which I had no issue with, considering we didn't get a match fee.

The infamous 2007 shoulder barge on Abdool Samad.

This is my final piece of advice. We all make mistakes - in life and on the cricket field.

So, when a fielder drops a catch off your bowling, don't take it out on them. Forget glaring at them while adopting the old Allan Border teapot stance - like Stuart Broad often does.

Do these same fielders treat you with the same discord when you bowl a long-hop or a leg stump half-volley?

I played a game for Scotland where a frustrated bowler screamed the name of a teammate who dropped a catch at short cover.

The following ball, the same bowler was smacked for a boundary when he attempted to dig in a bouncer.

Did the fielder who had just copped the tirade comment? No.

I've had many catches dropped off my bowling. It's disappointing, sure, but the moment has passed. Go back to your mark and get on with the game. If you do take a wicket, then you can have a cheeky, light-hearted dig at them.

Always treat your teammates with respect.

The same goes for the opposition. One of my pet hates is watching fast bowlers toil against top batsmen, going wicketless and getting hit around the park. Then, when the tailenders come in, they suddenly begin 'chirping' after saying jot to previous specialist batsmen. Some players can't help sledging - it's part of their personality. You could argue that sledging worked for someone like Glenn McGrath because from the outside it seemed to help him reach the intensity required, even though it appeared cringeworthy at times.

Off the field, McGrath is one of the nicest blokes you'd ever meet, so it was clear that having a 'word' to the batsmen helped him obtain that bit of 'mongrel' he wanted.

> *"Don't do that too often otherwise*
> *his captain will take him off!"*

I wouldn't have described myself as a 'nasty' fast bowler. Far from it. I enjoyed the game too much and always had plenty of respect for the opposition. Aside from the shoulder barge, my only other moment of nastiness occurred in 1989, when I was playing for Rockhampton against Callide Valley in the Queensland mining town of Biloela.

In my third over I was hit through square leg for a boundary. The batsman at the non-striker's end, a ginger-haired bruiser by the name of Kevin Hogan, sledged me - indirectly. He shouted to his partner, "Don't do that too often otherwise his captain will take him off!" It was the first and only time I'd ever been sledged while bowling.

I was livid. Suddenly, I had that 'mongrel' instinct. I wasn't going to bowl within myself anymore. I wanted to hurt Hogan, not get him out. Two balls later, Hogan was on strike. Predictably, I bounced him and struck him just above his left eye, splitting him open. He collapsed to the ground clutching his head, with blood pouring out onto the pitch. Hogan was helped from the pitch and taken to hospital to get stitched up.

The most bizarre part about this story is that about five hours later, I had to pad up to bat, but I didn't have any pads. There was a scattering of equipment around the clubhouse, so I managed to find a pair of pads.

Whilst I was batting, I noticed that Hogan had returned from hospital with a bandage wrapped around his head. I also noticed his blood that had stained the pitch, and I began to feel quite bad about what I had done.

After my partner hit the winning runs, we walked off and shook hands with the Callide Valley players. I walked over to Hogan and offered my hand, to which he grumbled, "You're wearing my pads."

Kevin Hogan was tough-as-nails, a typical country cricketer who was raised on a cattle property in the heat of Central Queensland. He wasn't the prettiest of batsmen, but he was a bloke who could bat forever if he had to. He was never shy of a word either.

On this occasion, I got the better of him, but there were other times where he was the epitome of the 'immovable object'. Sadly, Hogan passed away a few years back.

When coaches talk about being aggressive, they don't want you to suddenly start abusing batsmen, or trying to bounce them every ball. Cricket's not about that - not since 'sandpaper-gate' anyway.

"Ian Healy sledged me once - well, it was more of a 'get lost' comment..."

'Aggressive bowling' is bowling *at* the batsmen, not giving them a chance to rest or leave balls alone. It doesn't mean that we have to resort to 'bodyline' as often as possible.

It's about making the batsmen work for their runs and portraying a body language that demonstrates dominance and confidence - a similar mindset to a batsman who is always looking for runs - whether it's a quick single or running three instead of two. Aggressive bowling is also about finding out a batsmen's weakness and relentlessly targeting that weakness.

I never sledged when bowling. It seemed a little bit silly if I'm honest. Humourous banter? Fair enough, but not sledging.

Ian Healy sledged me once - well, it was more of a 'get lost' comment inside a Rockhampton nightclub called Flamingo's. In January 1990, Queensland had defeated Sri Lanka in a 50 over game. Many of the players were out 'on the town', so my mates and I thought we'd join them. Later in the evening, I asked Ian Healy who the fastest bowler in Australia was.

"Merv," he replied.

I then wanted to ask him who was the fastest bowler he had faced, but he cut me off before I could finish the question.

"Mate, I've already answered your question."

I can understand the wicket-keeping legend was probably grumpy. It had been hot. Very hot. Rockhampton is always baking in the summer.

As well as that, I was probably like pesky fruit fly in that dark night-club, desperate to engage in some chat with some cricketing heroes. However, I never forgot about that experience with Healy.

Because of this, when I played at the county grounds in England, I signed every bat and shirt. I spoke to the fans and tried to answer their every question, no matter how banal. I didn't want anyone, especially a young fast bowler, feeling as disappointed as I did that night in Flamingos.

I've been sledged many times when batting.

In a game against Durham at the Grange in Edinburgh, former England paceman Graham Onions sledged me after firing down a bouncer which I ducked. Unfortunately, I couldn't understand a word he said, so I replied, "...pitch it up and let's see what you've got to say then!".

Joe Dawes, the ex-Queensland quick, sledged me when he was play-ing for Middlesex in 2004. I'd hit him for a few boundaries at a game in Richmond, London.

After smashing another one to the fence, he muttered something towards my direction, to which I responded, "Joe you make my shoes - I'm not saying a thing!".

When it comes to sledging, I always think of the great West Indian quicks: Marshall, Holding, Garner, Roberts, Ambrose and Walsh. They let the ball do the talking.

CONCLUSION

"A balanced approach, running at your optimum speed, with a controlled delivery stride will assist you more with rhythm and pace, compared to a frenetic run-up and rushed action."

Writing this book has been like bowling a marathon spell. There have been times where I've wanted to take a break. Then I hear Mike Whitney's booming voice - a vivid reminder about not giving up.

There have been times when I've been distracted. But, no matter what, I always looked forward to returning to the book, to share my knowledge of the skill and to reminisce about lifelong memories.

Bowling is like that. Tough stints are inevitable, but we love the challenge that bowling fast provides us. The physical challenge, the mental toughness required and the pure joy of getting batsmen out are what drives us on.

We know that if we bowl a bad delivery, we can make amends with the following ball. And, we know that we're the individual that brings the x-factor to a team, the unpredictability and in most cases, the charisma.

Dougie Brown was not a quick bowler, but he made the most of his ability through sheer determination and perseverance. To be a successful fast bowler, you must share that same work ethic - that same burning desire to keep improving.

From the technical side, I wrote in detail about working everything in straight lines - working your limbs in unison with your momentum aimed towards your target. Working in straight lines - from your run-up, your delivery and your follow-through - will add pace and decrease injury risk.

A balanced approach, running at your optimum speed, with a controlled delivery stride will assist you more with rhythm and pace, compared to a frenetic run-up and rushed action.

Be wary about changing your natural action. Tinker with it if you believe there will be a long-term benefit, but any adjustments have to be drip-fed. Step through your action, bowl into a side net and seek the advice of a coaching specialist. Gradually increase intensity as your body fine-tunes itself to modifications.

This technical side of bowling, coupled with specific physical activities and repetitive drills that mirror the rigours and performance of bowling quick, will add speed to your deliveries.

*Invest in a medicine ball and
when you run, adopt the mindset
of interval training to improve
your speed and stamina.*

But, be mindful of your workload between games. Be smart with the number of overs you bowl. The stress of constant crease pounding is damaging. The forces placed on your front foot are between five to ten times your body weight.

Therefore, you must strike the delicate balance of bowling enough overs to keep your rhythm ticking over, but not so many that your body suffers. Don't bowl more than eight overs in a training session - if anything, bowl less.

Get into the habit of using the gym to work your bowling muscles and place less stress on your limbs. Invest in a medicine ball and when you run, adopt the mindset of interval training to improve your speed and stamina. Remember, what you do in training should mirror the physical demands of bowling fast. High-intensity interval training is the key.

Whilst mental toughness and physical prowess are fundamental to a fast bowler; they're somewhat useless if you don't have accuracy or skill. These abilities are a bit like the skill of reading for a young student. Unless they can read, every school subject will be a challenge.

"Keep thinking on your feet during the game - the greatest quicks always did. Consider the boundary sizes and the pace of the pitch. Communicate with your skipper and adjust your plans accordingly."

Take particular care with your grip. The grip plays a large part in maintaining accuracy and adding pace. Get the bowling fingers and wrist behind the ball.

Accuracy is obtained by working limbs in straight lines towards the target, as well as repetitive drills aimed at a small channel on the pitch.

There are many different grips which I have outlined in this book. Try them at practice. Use the width of the crease to increase your chances of taking wickets.

Learn from the modifications that Stuart Broad has made to his delivery position, where batsmen are forced to play at nearly every ball. This is aggressive, attacking bowling.

On the pitch, always have a plan, particularly when bowling to aggressive opening batsmen, and during the death overs.

The key here is to maintain a clear thought process and to practice your death bowling tactics at training. The general consensus from current and former professional batsmen is that the most difficult ball to face is the wide off stump yorker or low full toss, with a wide third man, a deep point or deep cover and a long-off.

This strategy, combined with a straight yorker, selective pace variations and a back of a length delivery that offers no width should form your base plan for the death overs.

Keep thinking on your feet during the game - the greatest quicks always did. Consider the boundary sizes and the pace of the pitch. Communicate with your skipper and adjust your plans accordingly.

Take nutrition seriously - be mindful of your diet, particularly in the evening and morning of a game. Adapt a professional and disciplined mantra, on and off the field.

Finally, look after your feet and invest in a good pair of light, yet supportive bowling boots with personalised orthotics. Now, you're set to take the new ball.

ACKNOWLEDGEMENT

Thank you to the following individuals who helped with the publication and material in this book.

Josh Johnstone
Suresh Balkrishna
John Blain
Dougie Brown
Qasim Sheikh - ("Sheiky's Sports Journey's" podcast youtube channel)
Sikandar Raza
Trent Woodhill
Ed Cowan
Yasir Arafat
Calum MacLeod
Kyle Coetzer
George Munsey
Gavin Hamilton
Billy McPate
Mac Wylie
Bob Cottom
Shane Burger
Libby Robinson
Jen Clifford
Craig Hoffmann
Tony Hoffmann
Lynette Hoffmann

Cricket Scotland
Donald MacLeod (www.donald-macleod.com)
David Potter (@DMP_Dunfermline)
Barry Chambers (www.cricketeurope.com)

ABOUT THE AUTHOR

Paul Hoffmann

Paul Hoffmann was born in the country town of Rockhampton in Queensland, Australia.

He represented Australia Country in 1993, before spending three seasons at Manly Warringah Cricket Club in Sydney, where he was also a part of the New South Wales Sheffield Shield squad.

In 1997 Hoffmann signed for Uddingston Cricket Club in Scotland, and has remained there for the best part of 20 years.

During this time, Hoffmann was capped 119 times for Scotland, and in 2017, he was inducted into the Cricket Scotland Hall of Fame.

A keen student of the game, Hoffmann is an ECB Level 2 coach, and enjoys nothing more than passing on his expertise to aspiring fast bowlers.

BOOKS BY THIS AUTHOR

Survival Guide For New Teachers

Teaching is a challenging job, but for beginning teachers, it's even more demanding. A significant percentage of teachers quit within their first two years. Paul Hoffmann was nearly one of those teachers.

In 'Survival Guide for New Teachers', Hoffmann talks candidly about the tough times, when he was on the verge of quitting the profession.

With a down to earth approach, the Scottish based Australian draws on his personal experiences, from the good and the bad, to help drive a message of resilience and positivity for new teachers.

He recalls anecdotes from his training and probationary years that will not only make you laugh, but make you coil with anger and disbelief.

Hoffmann shares coping strategies throughout the book's 10 chapters, including: dealing with poor behaviour, workload management, effective use of resources, pupil engagement and mental health. The book also includes tips and advice from teachers and Headteachers from Australia and the United Kingdom.

The life of a beginning teacher is stressful, but often very rewarding. There will be student and probationary teachers out there full of nervous anticipation about what lies ahead.

'Survival Guide for New Teachers' could well be their saviour.

MISCELLANEOUS

Image 1: First sketch of cover idea given to Josh Johnstone.
Image 2: 1981 Queensland representative.
Image 3: First Scotland playing top. This team included overseas professionals Jon Kent and India's very own Rahul Dravid.
Image 4: 2007 World Cup action portrait by East Kilbride artist Craig Smith, purchased by Sir Boyd Tunnock at the Uddingston Cricket Club dinner in 2020.

Printed in Great Britain
by Amazon

72877937R00129